Java SE 8 for the Really Impatient

Java SE 8
for the Really Impatient

Cay S. Horstmann

✦✦Addison-Wesley

Upper Saddle River, NJ • Boston • Indianapolis • San Francisco
New York • Toronto • Montreal • London • Munich • Paris • Madrid
Capetown • Sydney • Tokyo • Singapore • Mexico City

For information about buying this title in bulk quantities, or for special sales opportunities (which may include electronic versions; custom cover designs; and content particular to your business, training goals, marketing focus, or branding interests), please contact our corporate sales department at corpsales@pearsoned.com or (800) 382-3419.

For government sales inquiries, please contact governmentsales@pearsoned.com.

For questions about sales outside the United States, please contact international@pearsoned.com.

Visit us on the Web: informit.com/aw

Library of Congress Cataloging-in-Publication Data

Horstmann, Cay S., 1959-
  Java SE 8 for the really impatient / Cay S. Horstmann.
      pages cm
  Includes index.
  ISBN-13: 978-0-321-92776-7 (pbk. : alk. paper)
  ISBN-10: 0-321-92776-1 (pbk. : alk. paper)
  1. Java (Computer program language) 2. Computer programming. 3. Computer platform. I. Title.
  QA76.73.J38H675447 2014
  005.2'762—dc23

                                                                    2013046266

ISBN-13: 978-0-321-92776-7
ISBN-10: 0-321-92776-1
Text printed in the United States on recycled paper at RR Donnelley in Crawfordsville, Indiana.
Second printing, December 2014

To Greg Doench, my editor for two decades, whose patience, kindness, and good judgment I greatly admire

Contents

Preface

This book gives a concise introduction to the many new features of Java 8 (and a few features of Java 7 that haven't received much attention) for programmers who are already familiar with Java.

This book is written in the "impatient" style that I first tried out in a book called *Scala for the Impatient*. In that book, I wanted to quickly cut to the chase without lecturing the reader about the superiority of one paradigm over another. I presented information in small chunks organized to help you quickly retrieve it when needed. The approach was a big success in the Scala community, and I am employing it again in this book.

With Java 8, the Java programming language and library receive a major refresh. Lambda expressions make it possible to write "snippets of computations" in a concise way, so that you can pass them to other code. The recipient can choose to execute your computation when appropriate and as often as appropriate. This has a profound impact on building libraries.

In particular, working with collections has completely changed. Instead of specifying how to compute a result ("traverse from the beginning to the end, and if an element matches a condition, compute a value from it, and add that value to a sum"), you specify what you want ("give me the sum of all elements that match a condition"). The library is then able to reorder the computation—for example, to take advantage of parallelism. Or, if you just want to have the first hundred matches, it can stop the computation without you having to maintain a counter.

The brand-new *stream* API of Java 8 puts this idea to work. In the first chapter, you learn all about the syntax of lambda expressions, and Chapter 2 gives a complete overview of streams. In Chapter 3, I provide you with tips on how to effectively design your own libraries with lambdas.

With Java 8, developers of client-side applications need to transition to the JavaFX API since Swing is now in "maintenance mode." Chapter 4 gives a quick introduction to JavaFX for a programmer who needs to put together a graphical program—when a picture speaks louder than 1,000 strings.

Having waited for far too many years, programmers are finally able to use a well-designed date/time library. Chapter 5 covers the java.time API in detail.

Each version of Java brings enhancements in the concurrency API, and Java 8 is no exception. In Chapter 6, you learn about improvements in atomic counters, concurrent hash maps, parallel array operations, and composable futures.

Java 8 bundles Nashorn, a high-quality JavaScript implementation. In Chapter 7, you will see how to execute JavaScript on the Java Virtual Machine, and how to interoperate with Java code.

Chapter 8 collects miscellaneous smaller, but nevertheless useful, features of Java 8. Chapter 9 does the same for Java 7, focusing on improved exception handling, the "new I/O" enhancements for working with files and directories, and other library enhancements that you may have missed.

My thanks go, as always, to my editor Greg Doench, who had the idea of a short book that brings experienced programmers up to speed with Java 8. Dmitry Kirsanov and Alina Kirsanova once again turned an XHTML manuscript into an attractive book with amazing speed and attention to detail. I am grateful to the reviewers who spotted many embarrassing errors and gave excellent suggestions for improvement. They are: Gail Anderson, Paul Anderson, James Denvir, Trisha Gee, Brian Goetz (special thanks for the very thorough review), Marty Hall, Angelika Langer, Mark Lawrence, Stuart Marks, Attila Szegedi, and Jim Weaver.

I hope that you enjoy reading this concise introduction to the new features of Java 8, and that it will make you a more successful Java programmer. If you find errors or have suggestions for improvement, please visit http://horstmann.com/java8 and leave a comment. On that page, you will also find a link to an archive file containing all code examples from the book.

Cay Horstmann
San Francisco, 2013

About the Author

Cay S. Horstmann is the author of *Scala for the Impatient* (Addison-Wesley, 2012), is principal author of *Core Java™, Volumes I and II, Ninth Edition* (Prentice Hall, 2013), and has written a dozen other books for professional programmers and computer science students. He is a professor of computer science at San Jose State University and is a Java Champion.

Lambda Expressions

Topics in This Chapter

Chapter 1

Java was designed in the 1990s as an object-oriented programming language, when object-oriented programming was the principal paradigm for software development. Long before there was object-oriented programming, there were functional programming languages such as Lisp and Scheme, but their benefits were not much appreciated outside academic circles. Recently, functional programming has risen in importance because it is well suited for concurrent and event-driven (or "reactive") programming. That doesn't mean that objects are bad. Instead, the winning strategy is to blend object-oriented and functional programming. This makes sense even if you are not interested in concurrency. For example, collection libraries can be given powerful APIs if the language has a convenient syntax for function expressions.

The principal enhancement in Java 8 is the addition of functional programming constructs to its object-oriented roots. In this chapter, you will learn the basic syntax. The next chapter shows you how to put that syntax to use with Java collections, and in Chapter 3 you will learn how to build your own functional libraries.

The key points of this chapter are:

- A lambda expression is a block of code with parameters.

- Use a lambda expression whenever you want a block of code executed at a later point in time.

- Lambda expressions can be converted to functional interfaces.

- Lambda expressions can access effectively final variables from the enclosing scope.

- Method and constructor references refer to methods or constructors without invoking them.

- You can now add default and static methods to interfaces that provide concrete implementations.

- You must resolve any conflicts between default methods from multiple interfaces.

1.1 Why Lambdas?

A "lambda expression" is a block of code that you can pass around so it can be executed later, once or multiple times. Before getting into the syntax (or even the curious name), let's step back and see where you have used similar code blocks in Java all along.

When you want to do work in a separate thread, you put the work into the run method of a Runnable, like this:

```
class Worker implements Runnable {
   public void run() {
      for (int i = 0; i < 1000; i++)
         doWork();
   }
   ...
}
```

Then, when you want to execute this code, you construct an instance of the Worker class. You can then submit the instance to a thread pool, or, to keep it simple, start a new thread:

```
Worker w = new Worker();
new Thread(w).start();
```

The key point is that the run method contains code that you want to execute in a separate thread.

Or consider sorting with a custom comparator. If you want to sort strings by length instead of the default dictionary order, you can pass a Comparator object to the sort method:

Comparator⟨T⟩
is an intuface
that declares
public int compare(s1,s2)

```
class LengthComparator implements Comparator<String> {
   public int compare(String first, String second) {
      return Integer.compare(first.length(), second.length());
   }
}
```

```
Arrays.sort(strings, new LengthComparator());
```

The sort method keeps calling the compare method, rearranging the elements if they are out of order, until the array is sorted. You give the sort method a snippet of code needed to compare elements, and that code is integrated into the rest of the sorting logic, which you'd probably not care to reimplement.

 NOTE: The call Integer.compare(x, y) returns zero if x and y are equal, a negative number if x < y, and a positive number if x > y. This static method has been added to Java 7 (see Chapter 9). Note that you shouldn't compute x - y to compare x and y since that computation can overflow for large operands of opposite sign.

As another example for deferred execution, consider a button callback. You put the callback action into a method of a class implementing the listener interface, construct an instance, and register the instance with the button. That happens so often that many programmers use the "anonymous instance of anonymous class" syntax:

```
button.setOnAction(new EventHandler<ActionEvent>() {
    public void handle(ActionEvent event) {
        System.out.println("Thanks for clicking!");
    }
});
```

What matters is the code inside the handle method. That code is executed whenever the button is clicked.

 NOTE: Since Java 8 positions JavaFX as the successor to the Swing GUI toolkit, I use JavaFX in these examples. (See Chapter 4 for more information on JavaFX.) Of course, the details don't matter. In every user interface toolkit, be it Swing, JavaFX, or Android, you give a button some code that you want to run when the button is clicked.

In all three examples, you saw the same approach. A block of code was passed to someone—a thread pool, a sort method, or a button. The code was called at some later time.

Up to now, giving someone a block of code hasn't been easy in Java. You couldn't just pass code blocks around. Java is an object-oriented language, so you had to construct an object belonging to a class that has a method with the desired code.

In other languages, it is possible to work with blocks of code directly. The Java designers have resisted adding this feature for a long time. After all, a great

[handwritten margin notes: In Java, you pass objects of classes implementing certain functions]

[handwritten margin notes: All Java APIs handle objects]

strength of Java is its simplicity and consistency. A language can become an un-maintainable mess if it includes every feature that yields marginally more concise code. However, in those other languages it isn't just easier to spawn a thread or to register a button click handler; large swaths of their APIs are simpler, more consistent, and more powerful. In Java, one could have written similar APIs that take objects of classes implementing a particular function, but such APIs would be unpleasant to use.

For some time now, the question was not whether to augment Java for functional programming, but how to do it. It took several years of experimentation before a design emerged that is a good fit for Java. In the next section, you will see how you can work with blocks of code in Java 8.

1.2 The Syntax of Lambda Expressions

Consider again the sorting example from the preceding section. We pass code that checks whether one string is shorter than another. We compute

[handwritten margin note: Comparator]

```
Integer.compare(first.length(), second.length())
```

What are first and second? They are both strings. Java is a strongly typed language, and we must specify that as well:

```
(String first, String second)
   -> Integer.compare(first.length(), second.length())
```

You have just seen your first *lambda expression*. Such an expression is simply a block of code, together with the specification of any variables that must be passed to the code.

Why the name? Many years ago, before there were any computers, the logician Alonzo Church wanted to formalize what it means for a mathematical function to be effectively computable. (Curiously, there are functions that are known to exist, but nobody knows how to compute their values.) He used the Greek letter lambda (λ) to mark parameters. Had he known about the Java API, he would have written

```
λfirst.λsecond.Integer.compare(first.length(), second.length())
```

 NOTE: Why the letter λ? Did Church run out of other letters of the alphabet? Actually, the venerable *Principia Mathematica* used the ^ accent to denote free variables, which inspired Church to use an uppercase lambda Λ for parameters. But in the end, he switched to the lowercase version. Ever since, an expression with parameter variables has been called a lambda expression.

You have just seen one form of lambda expressions in Java: parameters, the ->
arrow, and an expression. If the code carries out a computation that doesn't fit
in a single expression, write it exactly like you would have written a method:
enclosed in {} and with explicit return statements. For example,

```
(String first, String second) -> {
    if (first.length() < second.length()) return -1;
    else if (first.length() > second.length()) return 1;
    else return 0;
}
```

only method references can omit a parameter signature

If a lambda expression has no parameters, you still supply empty parentheses,
just as with a parameterless method:

good use of no parens

```
() -> { for (int i = 0; i < 1000; i++) doWork(); }
```

If the parameter types of a lambda expression can be inferred, you can omit them.
For example,

```
Comparator<String> comp
    = (first, second) // Same as (String first, String second)
        -> Integer.compare(first.length(), second.length());
```

Here, the compiler can deduce that first and second must be strings because the
lambda expression is assigned to a string comparator. (We will have a closer look
at this assignment in the next section.)

If a method has a single parameter with inferred type, you can even omit the
parentheses:

Num(inferred type) params:

0 - ()
1 - event
2 - (a, b)

```
EventHandler<ActionEvent> listener = event ->
    System.out.println("Thanks for clicking!");
    // Instead of (event) -> or (ActionEvent event) ->
```

> NOTE: You can add annotations or the final modifier to lambda parameters
> in the same way as for method parameters:
>
> ```
> (final String name) -> ...
> (@NonNull String name) -> ...
> ```

You never specify the result type of a lambda expression. It is always inferred
from context. For example, the expression

```
(String first, String second) -> Integer.compare(first.length(), second.length())
```

can be used in a context where a result of type int is expected.

> NOTE: It is illegal for a lambda expression to return a value in some branches but not in others. For example, `(int x) -> { if (x >= 0) return 1; }` is invalid.

1.3 Functional Interfaces

As we discussed, there are many existing interfaces in Java that encapsulate blocks of code, such as Runnable or Comparator. Lambdas are backwards compatible with these interfaces.

You can supply a lambda expression whenever an object of an interface with a single abstract method is expected. Such an interface is called a *functional interface*.

> NOTE: You may wonder why a functional interface must have a single *abstract* method. Aren't all methods in an interface abstract? Actually, it has always been possible for an interface to redeclare methods from the Object class such as toString or clone, and these declarations do not make the methods abstract. (Some interfaces in the Java API redeclare Object methods in order to attach javadoc comments. Check out the Comparator API for an example.) More importantly, as you will see in Section 1.7, "Default Methods," on page 14, in Java 8, interfaces can declare nonabstract methods.

With Java 8, Java provides APIs that make it easy to reason about our code in a functional way, but is creating objects and classes under-the-hood

To demonstrate the conversion to a functional interface, consider the Arrays.sort method. Its second parameter requires an instance of Comparator, an interface with a single method. Simply supply a lambda:

```
Arrays.sort(words,
    (first, second) -> Integer.compare(first.length(), second.length()));
```

Behind the scenes, the Arrays.sort method receives an object of some class that implements Comparator<String>. Invoking the compare method on that object executes the body of the lambda expression. The management of these objects and classes is completely implementation dependent, and it can be much more efficient than using traditional inner classes. It is best to think of a lambda expression as a function, not an object, and to accept that it can be converted to a functional interface.

This conversion to interfaces is what makes lambda expressions so compelling. The syntax is short and simple. Here is another example:

```
button.setOnAction(event ->
    System.out.println("Thanks for clicking!"));
```

That's a lot easier to read than the alternative with inner classes.

Java does not support function literals, but does do lambda expressions

In fact, conversion to a functional interface is the *only* thing that you can do with a lambda expression in Java. In other programming languages that support function literals, you can declare function types such as (String, String) -> int, declare variables of those types, and use the variables to save function expressions. However, the Java designers decided to stick with the familiar concept of interfaces instead of adding function types to the language.

lambda expressions ONLY map to functional interfaces!

> NOTE: You can't even assign a lambda expression to a variable of type
> Object—Object is not a functional interface.

The Java API defines a number of very generic functional interfaces in the java.util.function package. (We will have a closer look at these interfaces in Chapters 2 and 3.) One of the interfaces, BiFunction<T, U, R>, describes functions with parameter types T and U and return type R. You can save our string comparison lambda in a variable of that type:

But, we have interfaces to emulate it[en] behavior

```
BiFunction<String, String, Integer> comp
    = (first, second) -> Integer.compare(first.length(), second.length());
```

However, that does not help you with sorting. There is no Arrays.sort method that wants a BiFunction. If you have used a functional programming language before, you may find this curious. But for Java programmers, it's pretty natural. An interface such as Comparator has a specific purpose, not just a method with given parameter and return types. Java 8 retains this flavor. When you want to do something with lambda expressions, you still want to keep the purpose of the expression in mind, and have a specific functional interface for it.

"purpose" of an expression

The interfaces in java.util.function are used in several Java 8 APIs, and you will likely see them elsewhere in the future. But keep in mind that you can equally well convert a lambda expression into a functional interface that is a part of whatever API you use today.

interfaces != object

> NOTE: You can tag any functional interface with the @FunctionalInterface an-
> notation. This has two advantages. The compiler checks that the annotated
> entity is an interface with a single abstract method. And the javadoc page
> includes a statement that your interface is a functional interface.
>
> It is not required to use the annotation. Any interface with a single
> abstract method is, by definition, a functional interface. But using the
> @FunctionalInterface annotation is a good idea.

Finally, note that checked exceptions matter when a lambda is converted to an instance of a functional interface. If the body of a lambda expression may throw a checked exception, that exception needs to be declared in the abstract method of the target interface. For example, the following would be an error:

```
Runnable sleeper = () -> { System.out.println("Zzz"); Thread.sleep(1000); };
    // Error: Thread.sleep can throw a checked InterruptedException
```

Since the `Runnable.run` cannot throw any exception, this assignment is illegal. To fix the error, you have two choices. You can catch the exception in the body of the lambda expression. Or assign the lambda to an interface whose single abstract method can throw the exception. For example, the `call` method of the `Callable` interface can throw any exception. Therefore, you can assign the lambda to a `Callable<Void>` (if you add a statement `return null`).

1.4 Method References   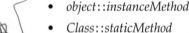 Syntactic sugar for lambdas!

Sometimes, there is already a method that carries out exactly the action that you'd like to pass on to some other code. For example, suppose you simply want to print the event object whenever a button is clicked. Of course, you could call

```
button.setOnAction(event -> System.out.println(event));
```

It would be nicer if you could just pass the `println` method to the `setOnAction` method. Here is how you do that:

```
button.setOnAction(System.out::println);
```

The expression `System.out::println` is a *method reference* that is equivalent to the lambda expression `x -> System.out.println(x)`.

As another example, suppose you want to sort strings regardless of letter case. You can pass this method reference:

```
Arrays.sort(strings, String::compareToIgnoreCase)
```

As you can see from these examples, the `::` operator separates the method name from the name of an object or class. There are three principal cases:

- *object*`::`*instanceMethod*
- *Class*`::`*staticMethod*
- *Class*`::`*instanceMethod*

In the first two cases, the method reference is equivalent to a lambda expression that supplies the parameters of the method. As already mentioned, `System.out::println` is equivalent to `x -> System.out.println(x)`. Similarly, `Math::pow` is equivalent to `(x, y) -> Math.pow(x, y)`.

 In the third case, the first parameter becomes the target of the method. For example, `String::compareToIgnoreCase` is the same as `(x, y) -> x.compareToIgnoreCase(y)`.

NOTE: When there are multiple overloaded methods with the same name, the compiler will try to find from the context which one you mean. For example, there are two versions of the Math.max method, one for integers and one for double values. Which one gets picked depends on the method parameters of the functional interface to which Math::max is converted. Just like lambda expressions, method references don't live in isolation. They are always turned into instances of functional interfaces.

lambdas are turned into instances of functional interfaces

You can invoke a method of an enclosing class or its superclass. For example, this::equals is the same as x -> this.equals(x). It is also valid to use super. The method reference

    super::instanceMethod

uses this as the target and invokes the superclass version of the given method. Here is an artificial example that shows the mechanics:

```
class Greeter {       not simple.
    public void greet() {
        System.out.println("Hello, world!");
    }
}

class ConcurrentGreeter extends Greeter {
    public void greet() {
        Thread t = new Thread(super::greet);
        t.start();
    }
}
```

When the thread starts, its Runnable is invoked, and super::greet is executed, calling the greet method of the superclass.

NOTE: In an inner class, you can capture the this reference of an enclosing class as *EnclosingClass*.this::*method* or *EnclosingClass*.super::*method*.

1.5 Constructor References

Constructor references are just like method references, except that the name of the method is new. For example, Button::new is a reference to a Button constructor. Which constructor? It depends on the context. Suppose you have a list of strings. Then you can turn it into an array of buttons, by calling the constructor on each of the strings, with the following invocation:

```
List<String> labels = ...;
Stream<Button> stream = labels.stream().map(Button::new);
List<Button> buttons = stream.collect(Collectors.toList());
```

We will discuss the details of the stream, map, and collect methods in Chapter 2. For now, what's important is that the map method calls the Button(String) constructor for each list element. There are multiple Button constructors, but the compiler picks the one with a String parameter because it infers from the context that the constructor is called with a string.

You can form constructor references with array types. For example, int[]::new is a constructor reference with one parameter: the length of the array. It is equivalent to the lambda expression x -> new int[x].

Array constructor references are useful to overcome a limitation of Java. It is not possible to construct an array of a generic type T. The expression new T[n] is an error since it would be erased to new Object[n]. That is a problem for library authors. For example, suppose we want to have an array of buttons. The Stream interface has a toArray method that returns an Object array:

```
Object[] buttons = stream.toArray();
```

But that is unsatisfactory. The user wants an array of buttons, not objects. The stream library solves that problem with constructor references. Pass Button[]::new to the toArray method:

```
Button[] buttons = stream.toArray(Button[]::new);
```

The toArray method invokes this constructor to obtain an array of the correct type. Then it fills and returns the array.

1.6 Variable Scope

Often, you want to be able to access variables from an enclosing method or class in a lambda expression. Consider this example:

```
public static void repeatMessage(String text, int count) {
    Runnable r = () -> {
        for (int i = 0; i < count; i++) {
            System.out.println(text);
            Thread.yield();
        }
    };
    new Thread(r).start();
}
```

Consider a call

```
repeatMessage("Hello", 1000); // Prints Hello 1,000 times in a separate thread
```

Now look at the variables count and text inside the lambda expression. Note that these variables are *not* defined in the lambda expression. Instead, these are parameter variables of the repeatMessage method.

If you think about it, something nonobvious is going on here. The code of the lambda expression may run long after the call to repeatMessage has returned and the parameter variables are gone. How do the text and count variables stay around?

To understand what is happening, we need to refine our understanding of a lambda expression. A lambda expression has three ingredients:

1. A block of code

2. Parameters

3. Values for the *free* variables, that is, the variables that are not parameters and not defined inside the code

In our example, the lambda expression has two free variables, text and count. The data structure representing the lambda expression must store the values for these variables, in our case, "Hello" and 1000. We say that these values have been *captured* by the lambda expression. (It's an implementation detail how that is done. For example, one can translate a lambda expression into an object with a single method, so that the values of the free variables are copied into instance variables of that object.)

 NOTE: The technical term for a block of code together with the values of the free variables is a *closure.* If someone gloats that their language has closures, rest assured that Java has them as well. In Java, lambda expressions are closures. In fact, inner classes have been closures all along. Java 8 gives us closures with an attractive syntax.

As you have seen, a lambda expression can capture the value of a variable in the enclosing scope. In Java, to ensure that the captured value is well-defined, there is an important restriction. In a lambda expression, you can only reference variables whose value doesn't change. For example, the following is illegal:

```
public static void repeatMessage(String text, int count) {
   Runnable r = () -> {
      while (count > 0) {
         count--; // Error: Can't mutate captured variable
         System.out.println(text);
         Thread.yield();
      }
   };
   new Thread(r).start();
}
```

There is a reason for this restriction. Mutating variables in a lambda expression is not threadsafe. Consider a sequence of concurrent tasks, each updating a shared counter.

```
int matches = 0;
for (Path p : files)
   new Thread(() -> { if (p has some property) matches++; }).start();
      // Illegal to mutate matches
```

If this code were legal, it would be very, very bad. The increment matches++ is not atomic, and there is no way of knowing what would happen if multiple threads execute that increment concurrently.

 NOTE: Inner classes can also capture values from an enclosing scope. Before Java 8, inner classes were only allowed to access final local variables. This rule has now been relaxed to match that for lambda expressions. An inner class can access any effectively final local variable—that is, any variable whose value does not change.

Don't count on the compiler to catch all concurrent access errors. The prohibition against mutation only holds for local variables. If matches is an instance or static variable of an enclosing class, then no error is reported, even though the result is just as undefined.

Also, it's perfectly legal to mutate a shared object, even though it is unsound. For example,

```
List<Path> matches = new ArrayList<>();
for (Path p : files)
   new Thread(() -> { if (p has some property) matches.add(p); }).start();
      // Legal to mutate matches, but unsafe
```

Note that the variable matches is *effectively final*. (An effectively final variable is a variable that is never assigned a new value after it has been initialized.) In our case, matches always refers to the same ArrayList object. However, the object is mutated, and that is not threadsafe. If multiple threads call add, the result is unpredictable.

"unpredictable"
↳ what happens?

There are safe mechanisms for counting and collecting values concurrently. In Chapter 2, you will see how to use streams to collect values with certain properties. In other situations, you may want to use threadsafe counters and collections. See Chapter 6 for more information on this important topic.

NOTE: As with inner classes, there is an escape hatch that lets a lambda expression update a counter in an enclosing local scope. Use an array of length 1, like this:

```
int[] counter = new int[1];
button.setOnAction(event -> counter[0]++);
```

Of course, code like this is not threadsafe. For a button callback, that doesn't matter, but in general, you should think twice before using this trick. You will see how to implement a threadsafe shared counter in Chapter 6.

The body of a lambda expression has *the same scope as a nested block*. The same rules for name conflicts and shadowing apply. It is illegal to declare a parameter or a local variable in the lambda that has the same name as a local variable.

```
Path first = Paths.get("/usr/bin");
Comparator<String> comp =
   (first, second) -> Integer.compare(first.length(), second.length());
   // Error: Variable first already defined
```

Inside a method, you can't have two local variables with the same name, and therefore, you can't introduce such variables in a lambda expression either.

When you use the this keyword in a lambda expression, you refer to the this parameter of the method that creates the lambda. For example, consider

```
public class Application {
   public void doWork() {
      Runnable runner = () -> { ...; System.out.println(this.toString()); ... };
      ...
   }
}
```

The expression this.toString() calls the toString method of the Application object, *not* the Runnable instance. There is nothing special about the use of this in a lambda expression. The scope of the lambda expression is nested inside the doWork method, and this has the same meaning anywhere in that method.

The "this" of a nested block

Solves backwards compatibility for Java interfaces

1.7 Default Methods

Many programming languages integrate function expressions with their collections library. This often leads to code that is shorter and easier to understand than the loop equivalent. For example, consider a loop

```
for (int i = 0; i < list.size(); i++)
   System.out.println(list.get(i));
```

There is a better way. The library designers can supply a forEach method that applies a function to each element. Then you can simply call

```
list.forEach(System.out::println);
```

That's fine if the collections library has been designed from the ground up. But the Java collections library has been designed many years ago, and there is a problem. If the Collection interface gets new methods, such as forEach, then every program that defines its own class implementing Collection will break until it, too, implements that method. That is simply unacceptable in Java.

The Java designers decided to solve this problem once and for all by allowing interface methods with concrete implementations (called *default methods*). Those methods can be safely added to existing interfaces. In this section, we'll look into default methods in detail.

Iterable ↓ Collection

 NOTE: In Java 8, the forEach method has been added to the Iterable interface, a superinterface of Collection, using the mechanism that I will describe in this section.

Consider this interface:

```
interface Person {
   long getId();
   default String getName() { return "John Q. Public"; }
}
```

The interface has two methods: getId, which is an abstract method, and the default method getName. A concrete class that implements the Person interface must, of course, provide an implementation of getId, but it can choose to keep the implementation of getName or to override it.

Default methods put an end to the classic pattern of providing an interface and an abstract class that implements most or all of its methods, such as Collection/AbstractCollection or WindowListener/WindowAdapter. Now you can just implement the methods in the interface.

What happens if the exact same method is defined as a default method in one interface and then again as a method of a superclass or another interface? Languages such as Scala and C++ have complex rules for resolving such ambiguities. Fortunately, the rules in Java are much simpler. Here they are:

1. Superclasses win. If a superclass provides a concrete method, default methods with the same name and parameter types are simply ignored.

2. Interfaces clash. If a superinterface provides a default method, and another interface supplies a method with the same name and parameter types (default or not), then you must resolve the conflict by overriding that method.

Let's look at the second rule. Consider another interface with a getName method:

```
interface Named {
    default String getName() { return getClass().getName() + "_" + hashCode(); }
}
```

What happens if you form a class that implements both of them?

```
class Student implements Person, Named {
    ...
}
```

The class inherits two inconsistent getName methods provided by the Person and Named interfaces. Rather than choosing one over the other, the Java compiler reports an error and leaves it up to the programmer to resolve the ambiguity. Simply provide a getName method in the Student class. In that method, you can choose one of the two conflicting methods, like this:

```
class Student implements Person, Named {
    public String getName() { return Person.super.getName(); }
    ...
}
```

Now assume that the Named interface does not provide a default implementation for getName:

```
interface Named {
    String getName();
}
```

Can the Student class inherit the default method from the Person interface? This might be reasonable, but the Java designers decided in favor of uniformity. It doesn't matter how two interfaces conflict. If at least one interface provides an implementation, the compiler reports an error, and the programmer must resolve the ambiguity.

NOTE: Of course, if neither interface provides a default for a shared method, then we are in the pre-Java 8 situation, and there is no conflict. An implementing class has two choices: implement the method, or leave it unimplemented. In the latter case, the class is itself abstract.

We just discussed name clashes between two interfaces. Now consider a class that extends a superclass and implements an interface, inheriting the same method from both. For example, suppose that `Person` is a class and `Student` is defined as

```
class Student extends Person implements Named { ... }
```

In that case, only the superclass method matters, and any default method from the interface is simply ignored. In our example, `Student` inherits the `getName` method from `Person`, and it doesn't make any difference whether the `Named` interface provides a default for `getName` or not. This is the "class wins" rule.

The "class wins" rule ensures compatibility with Java 7. If you add default methods to an interface, it has no effect on code that worked before there were default methods.

CAUTION: You can never make a default method that redefines one of the methods in the `Object` class. For example, you can't define a default method for `toString` or `equals`, even though that might be attractive for interfaces such as `List`. As a consequence of the "classes win" rule, such a method could never win against `Object.toString` or `Object.equals`.

1.8 Static Methods in Interfaces

As of Java 8, you are allowed to add static methods to interfaces. There was never a technical reason why this should be outlawed. It simply seemed to be against the spirit of interfaces as abstract specifications.

Up to now, it has been common to place static methods in companion classes. You find pairs of interfaces and utility classes such as `Collection`/`Collections` or `Path`/`Paths` in the standard library.

Have a look at the `Paths` class. It only has a couple of factory methods. You can construct a path from a sequence of strings, such as `Paths.get("jdk1.8.0", "jre", "bin")`. In Java 8, one could have added this method to the `Path` interface:

```
public interface Path {
   public static Path get(String first, String... more) {
      return FileSystems.getDefault().getPath(first, more);
   }
   ...
}
```

Then the Paths class is no longer necessary.

When you look at the Collections class, you will find two kinds of methods. A method such as

```
public static void shuffle(List<?> list)
```

would work well as a default method of the List interface

```
public default void shuffle()
```

You could then simply call list.shuffle() on any list.

For a factory method that doesn't work since you don't have an object on which to invoke the method. That is where static interface methods come in. For example,

```
public static <T> List<T> nCopies(int n, T o)
   // Constructs a list of n instances of o
```

could be a static method of the List interface. Then you would call List.nCopies(10, "Fred") instead of Collections.nCopies(10, "Fred") and it would be clear to the reader that the result is a List.

It is unlikely that the Java collections library will be refactored in this way, but when you implement your own interfaces, there is no longer a reason to provide a separate companion class for utility methods.

In Java 8, static methods have been added to quite a few interfaces. For example, the Comparator interface has a very useful static comparing method that accepts a "key extraction" function and yields a comparator that compares the extracted keys. To compare Person objects by name, use Comparator.comparing(Person::getName).

In this chapter, we have compared strings by length with the lambda expression (first, second) -> Integer.compare(first.length(), second.length()). But with the static compare method, we can do much better and simply use Comparator.comparing(String::length). This is a fitting way of closing this chapter because it demonstrates the power of working with functions. The compare method turns a function (the key extractor) into a more complex function (the key-based comparator). We will examine such "higher order functions" in more detail in Chapter 3.

Exercises

1. Is the comparator code in the Arrays.sort method called in the same thread as the call to sort or a different thread?

2. Using the listFiles(FileFilter) and isDirectory methods of the java.io.File class, write a method that returns all subdirectories of a given directory. Use a lambda expression instead of a FileFilter object. Repeat with a method reference.

3. Using the list(FilenameFilter) method of the java.io.File class, write a method that returns all files in a given directory with a given extension. Use a lambda expression, not a FilenameFilter. Which variables from the enclosing scope does it capture?

4. Given an array of File objects, sort it so that the directories come before the files, and within each group, elements are sorted by path name. Use a lambda expression, not a Comparator.

5. Take a file from one of your projects that contains a number of ActionListener, Runnable, or the like. Replace them with lambda expressions. How many lines did it save? Was the code easier to read? Were you able to use method references?

6. Didn't you always hate it that you had to deal with checked exceptions in a Runnable? Write a method uncheck that catches all checked exceptions and turns them into unchecked exceptions. For example,

    ```
    new Thread(uncheck(
        () -> { System.out.println("Zzz"); Thread.sleep(1000); })).start();
        // Look, no catch (InterruptedException)!
    ```

    Hint: Define an interface RunnableEx whose run method may throw any exceptions. Then implement public static Runnable uncheck(RunnableEx runner). Use a lambda expression inside the uncheck method.

    Why can't you just use Callable<Void> instead of RunnableEx?

7. Write a static method andThen that takes as parameters two Runnable instances and returns a Runnable that runs the first, then the second. In the main method, pass two lambda expressions into a call to andThen, and run the returned instance.

8. What happens when a lambda expression captures values in an enhanced for loop such as this one?

    ```
    String[] names = { "Peter", "Paul", "Mary" };
    List<Runnable> runners = new ArrayList<>();
    for (String name : names)
        runners.add(() -> System.out.println(name));
    ```

Is it legal? Does each lambda expression capture a different value, or do they all get the last value? What happens if you use a traditional loop for (int i = 0; i < names.length; i++)?

9. Form a subinterface Collection2 from Collection and add a default method void forEachIf(Consumer<T> action, Predicate<T> filter) that applies action to each element for which filter returns true. How could you use it?

10. Go through the methods of the Collections class. If you were king for a day, into which interface would you place each method? Would it be a default method or a static method?

11. Suppose you have a class that implements two interfaces I and J, each of which has a method void f(). Exactly what happens if f is an abstract, default, or static method of I and an abstract, default, or static method of J? Repeat where a class extends a superclass S and implements an interface I, each of which has a method void f().

12. In the past, you were told that it's bad form to add methods to an interface because it would break existing code. Now you are told that it's okay to add new methods, provided you also supply a default implementation. How safe is that? Describe a scenario where the new stream method of the Collection interface causes legacy code to fail compilation. What about binary compatibility? Will legacy code from a JAR file still run?

Review:

Type erasure

Race conditions w/ mutable vars

Method signature for Comparator.comparing

How Does the comparator interface allow for Static methods like Integer.compare?

The Stream API

Topics in This Chapter

Chapter

You define the process, leave scheduling details aside.

Streams are the key abstraction in Java 8 for processing collections of values and specifying what you want to have done, leaving the scheduling of operations to the implementation. For example, if you want to compute the average of the values of a certain method, you specify that you want to call the method on each element and get the average of the values. You leave it to the stream library to parallelize the operation, using multiple threads for computing sums and counts of each segment and combining the results.

The key points of this chapter are:

- Iterators imply a specific traversal strategy and prohibit efficient concurrent execution.

- You can create streams from collections, arrays, generators, or iterators.

- Use filter to select elements and map to transform elements.

- Other operations for transforming streams include limit, distinct, and sorted.

- To obtain a result from a stream, use a reduction operator such as count, max, min, findFirst, or findAny. Some of these methods return an Optional value.

- The Optional type is intended as a safe alternative to working with null values. To use it safely, take advantage of the ifPresent and orElse methods.

- You can collect stream results in collections, arrays, strings, or maps.

- The groupingBy and partitioningBy methods of the Collectors class allow you to split the contents of a stream into groups, and to obtain a result for each group.

- There are specialized streams for the primitive types int, long, and double.

- When you work with parallel streams, be sure to avoid side effects, and consider giving up ordering constraints.

- You need to be familiar with a small number of functional interfaces in order to use the stream library.

2.1 From Iteration to Stream Operations

When you process a collection, you usually iterate over its elements and do some work with each of them. For example, suppose we want to count all long words in a book. First, let's put them into a list:

```
String contents = new String(Files.readAllBytes(
    Paths.get("alice.txt")), StandardCharsets.UTF_8); // Read file into string
List<String> words = Arrays.asList(contents.split("[\\P{L}]+"));
    // Split into words; nonletters are delimiters
```

Now we are ready to iterate:

```
int count = 0;
for (String w : words) {
    if (w.length() > 12) count++;
}
```

What's wrong with it? Nothing really—except that it is hard to parallelize the code. That's where the Java 8 bulk operations come in. In Java 8, the same operation looks like this:

```
long count = words.stream().filter(w -> w.length() > 12).count();
```

The stream method yields a *stream* for the words list. The filter method returns another stream that contains only the words of length greater than twelve. The count method reduces that stream to a result.

A stream seems superficially similar to a collection, allowing you to transform and retrieve data. But there are significant differences:

1. A stream does not store its elements. They may be stored in an underlying collection or generated on demand.

2. Stream operations don't mutate their source. Instead, they return new streams that hold the result.

3. Stream operations are *lazy* when possible. This means they are not executed until their result is needed. For example, if you only ask for the first five long words instead of counting them all, then the filter method will stop filtering after the fifth match. As a consequence, you can even have infinite streams!

In this chapter, you will learn all about streams. Many people find stream expressions easier to read than the loop equivalents. Moreover, they can be easily parallelized. Here is how you count long words in parallel:

```
long count = words.parallelStream().filter(w -> w.length() > 12).count();
```

Simply changing stream into parallelStream allows the stream library to do the filtering and counting in parallel.

Streams follow the "what, not how" principle. In our stream example, we describe what needs to be done: get the long words and count them. We don't specify in which order, or in which thread, this should happen. In contrast, the loop at the beginning of this section specifies exactly how the computation should work, and thereby forgoes any chances of optimization.

"what, not how principle"

When you work with streams, you set up a pipeline of operations in three stages.

nice

1. You create a stream.

2. You specify *intermediate operations* for transforming the initial stream into others, in one or more steps.

3. You apply a *terminal operation* to produce a result. This operation forces the execution of the lazy operations that precede it. Afterwards, the stream can no longer be used.

In our example, the stream was created with the stream or parallelStream method. The filter method transformed it, and count was the terminal operation.

 NOTE: Stream operations are *not* executed on the elements in the order in which they are invoked on the streams. In our example, nothing happens until count is called. When the count method asks for the first element, then the filter method starts requesting elements, until it finds one that has length > 12.

In the next section, you will see how to create a stream. The subsequent three sections deal with stream transformations. They are followed by five sections on terminal operations.

2.2 Stream Creation

You have already seen that you can turn any collection into a stream with the stream method that Java 8 added to the Collection interface. If you have an array, use the static Stream.of method instead.

```
Stream<String> words = Stream.of(contents.split("[\\P{L}]+"));
   // split returns a String[] array
```

The of method has a varargs parameter, so you can construct a stream from any number of arguments:

```
Stream<String> song = Stream.of("gently", "down", "the", "stream");
```

Use Arrays.stream(array, from, to) to make stream from a part of an array.

To make a stream with no elements, use the static Stream.empty method:

```
Stream<String> silence = Stream.empty();
   // Generic type <String> is inferred; same as Stream.<String>empty()
```

The Stream interface has two static methods for making infinite streams. The generate method takes a function with no arguments (or, technically, an object of the Supplier<T> interface—see Section 2.14, "Functional Interfaces," on page 42). Whenever a stream value is needed, that function is called to produce a value. You can get a stream of constant values as

```
Stream<String> echos = Stream.generate(() -> "Echo");
```

or a stream of random numbers as

```
Stream<Double> randoms = Stream.generate(Math::random);
```

To produce infinite sequences such as 0 1 2 3 ..., use the iterate method instead. It takes a "seed" value and a function (technically, a UnaryOperator<T>), and repeatedly applies the function to the previous result. For example,

```
Stream<BigInteger> integers
   = Stream.iterate(BigInteger.ZERO, n -> n.add(BigInteger.ONE));
```

The first element in the sequence is the seed BigInteger.ZERO. The second element is f(seed), or 1 (as a big integer). The next element is f(f(seed)), or 2, and so on.

 NOTE: A number of methods that yield streams have been added to the API with the Java 8 release. For example, the Pattern class now has a method splitAsStream that splits a CharSequence by a regular expression. You can use the following statement to split a string into words:

```
Stream<String> words
   = Pattern.compile("[\\P{L}]+").splitAsStream(contents);
```

The static `Files.lines` method returns a `Stream` of all lines in a file. The `Stream` interface has `AutoCloseable` as a superinterface. When the `close` method is called on the stream, the underlying file is also closed. To make sure that this happens, it is best to use the Java 7 try-with-resources statement:

```
try (Stream<String> lines = Files.lines(path)) {
    Do something with lines
}
```

The stream, and the underlying file with it, will be closed when the `try` block exits normally or through an exception.

2.3 The `filter`, `map`, and `flatMap` Methods

A stream transformation reads data from a stream and puts the transformed data into another stream. You have already seen the `filter` transformation that yields a new stream with all elements that match a certain condition. Here, we transform a stream of strings into another stream containing only long words:

```
List<String> wordList = ...;
Stream<String> words = wordList.stream();
Stream<String> longWords = words.filter(w -> w.length() > 12);
```

The argument of `filter` is a `Predicate<T>`—that is, a function from `T` to `boolean`.

Often, you want to transform the values in a stream in some way. Use the `map` method and pass the function that carries out the transformation. For example, you can transform all words to lowercase like this:

```
Stream<String> lowercaseWords = words.map(String::toLowerCase);
```

Here, we used `map` with a method reference. Often, you will use a lambda expression instead:

```
Stream<Character> firstChars = words.map(s -> s.charAt(0));
```

The resulting stream contains the first character of each word.

When you use `map`, a function is applied to each element, and the return values are collected in a new stream. Now suppose that you have a function that returns not just one value but a stream of values, such as this one:

```
public static Stream<Character> characterStream(String s) {
    List<Character> result = new ArrayList<>();
    for (char c : s.toCharArray()) result.add(c);
    return result.stream();
}
```

For example, `characterStream("boat")` is the stream `['b', 'o', 'a', 't']`. Suppose you map this method on a stream of strings:

```
Stream<Stream<Character>> result = words.map(w -> characterStream(w));
```

You will get a stream of streams, like `[... ['y', 'o', 'u', 'r'], ['b', 'o', 'a', 't'], ...]` To flatten it out to a stream of characters `[... 'y', 'o', 'u', 'r', 'b', 'o', 'a', 't', ...]`, use the `flatMap` method instead of `map`:

```
Stream<Character> letters = words.flatMap(w -> characterStream(w))
    // Calls characterStream on each word and flattens the results
```

> NOTE: You may find a `flatMap` method in classes other than streams. It is a general concept in computer science. Suppose you have a generic type G (such as `Stream`) and functions f from some type T to $G<U>$ and g from U to $G<V>$. Then you can compose them, that is, first apply f and then g, by using `flatMap`. This is a key idea in the theory of *monads*. But don't worry—you can use `flatMap` without knowing anything about monads.

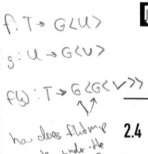

2.4 Extracting Substreams and Combining Streams

The call *stream*`.limit(n)` returns a new stream that ends after n elements (or when the original stream ends if it is shorter). This method is particularly useful for cutting infinite streams down to size. For example,

```
Stream<Double> randoms = Stream.generate(Math::random).limit(100);
```

yields a stream with 100 random numbers.

The call *stream*`.skip(n)` does the exact opposite. It discards the first n elements. This is handy in our book reading example where, due to the way the `split` method works, the first element is an unwanted empty string. We can make it go away by calling `skip`:

```
Stream<String> words = Stream.of(contents.split("[\\P{L}]+")).skip(1);
```

You can concatenate two streams with the static `concat` method of the `Stream` class:

```
Stream<Character> combined = Stream.concat(
    characterStream("Hello"), characterStream("World"));
    // Yields the stream ['H', 'e', 'l', 'l', 'o', 'W', 'o', 'r', 'l', 'd']
```

Of course, the first stream should not be infinite—otherwise the second wouldn't ever get a chance.

TIP: The peek method yields another stream with the same elements as the original, but a function is invoked every time an element is retrieved. That is handy for debugging:

```
Object[] powers = Stream.iterate(1.0, p -> p * 2)
    .peek(e -> System.out.println("Fetching " + e))
    .limit(20).toArray();
```

When an element is actually accessed, a message is printed. This way you can verify that the infinite stream returned by iterate is processed lazily.

2.5 Stateful Transformations

The stream transformations of the preceding sections were *stateless*. When an element is retrieved from a filtered or mapped stream, the answer does not depend on the previous elements. There are also a few stateful transformations. For example, the distinct method returns a stream that yields elements from the original stream, in the same order, except that duplicates are suppressed. The stream must obviously remember the elements that it has already seen.

```
Stream<String> uniqueWords
    = Stream.of("merrily", "merrily", "merrily", "gently").distinct();
    // Only one "merrily" is retained
```

The sorted method must see the entire stream and sort it before it can give out any elements—after all, the smallest one might be the last one. Clearly, you can't sort an infinite stream.

There are several sorted methods. One works for streams of Comparable elements, and another accepts a Comparator. Here, we sort strings so that the longest ones come first:

```
Stream<String> longestFirst =
    words.sorted(Comparator.comparing(String::length).reversed());
```

Of course, you can sort a collection without using streams. The sorted method is useful when the sorting process is a part of a stream pipeline.

 NOTE: The Collections.sort method sorts a collection in place, whereas Stream.sorted returns a new sorted stream.

my S. sorted (Comparator)

Collections. sort (my C)

my S. sorted (Comparator)

2.6 Simple Reductions

Now that you have seen how to create and transform streams, we will finally get to the most important point—getting answers from the stream data. The methods that we cover in this section are called *reductions*. They reduce the stream to a value that can be used in your program. Reductions are *terminal operations*. After a terminal operation has been applied, the stream ceases to be usable.

You have already seen a simple reduction: the count method that returns the number of elements of the stream.

Other simple reductions are max and min that return the largest or smallest value. There is a twist—these methods return an Optional<T> value that either wraps the answer or indicates that there is none (because the stream happened to be empty). In the olden days, it was common to return null in such a situation. But that can lead to null pointer exceptions when an unusual situation arises in an incompletely tested program. In Java 8, the Optional type is the preferred way of indicating a missing return value. We discuss the Optional type in detail in the next section. Here is how you can get the maximum of a stream:

```
Optional<String> largest = words.max(String::compareToIgnoreCase);
if (largest.isPresent())
    System.out.println("largest: " + largest.get());
```

The findFirst returns the first value in a nonempty collection. It is often useful when combined with filter. For example, here we find the first word that starts with the letter Q, if it exists:

```
Optional<String> startsWithQ
    = words.filter(s -> s.startsWith("Q")).findFirst();
```

can't use a method reference bc of the argument needed

If you are okay with any match, not just the first one, then use the findAny method. This is effective when you parallelize the stream since the first match in any of the examined segments will complete the computation.

```
Optional<String> startsWithQ
    = words.parallel().filter(s -> s.startsWith("Q")).findAny();
```

If you just want to know there is a match, use anyMatch. That method takes a predicate argument, so you won't need to use filter.

```
boolean aWordStartsWithQ
    = words.parallel().anyMatch(s -> s.startsWith("Q"));
```

There are also methods allMatch and noneMatch that return true if all or no elements match a predicate. These methods always examine the entire stream, but they still benefit from being run in parallel.

good for parallelization

2.7 The Optional Type

An Optional<T> object is either a wrapper for an object of type T or for no object. It is intended as a safer alternative than a reference of type T that refers to an object or null. But it is only safer if you use it right.

The get method gets the wrapped element if it exists, or throws a NoSuchElementException if it doesn't. Therefore,

```
Optional<T> optionalValue = ...;
optionalValue.get().someMethod()
```

is no safer than

```
T value = ...;
value.someMethod();
```

As you saw in the preceding section, the isPresent method reports whether an Optional<T> object has a value. But

```
if (optionalValue.isPresent()) optionalValue.get().someMethod();
```

is no easier than

```
if (value != null) value.someMethod();
```

In the next section, you will see how you should really work with Optional values.

2.7.1 Working with Optional Values

The key to using Optional effectively is to use a method that either *consumes the correct value* or *produces an alternative.*

Besides the isPresent method, there is an ifPresent method that accepts a function. If the optional value exists, it is passed to that function. Otherwise, nothing happens. Instead of using an if statement, you call

```
optionalValue.ifPresent(v -> Process v);
```

For example, if you want to add the value to a set if it is present, call

```
optionalValue.ifPresent(v -> results.add(v));
```
or simply

```
optionalValue.ifPresent(results::add);
```

When calling this version of ifPresent, no value is returned. If you want to process the result, use map instead:

```
Optional<Boolean> added = optionalValue.map(results::add);
```

Now added has one of three values: true or false wrapped into an Optional, if optionalValue was present, or an empty optional otherwise.

 NOTE: This map method is the analog of the map method of the Stream interface that you have seen in Section 2.3, "The filter, map, and flatMap Methods," on page 25. Simply imagine an optional value as a stream of size zero or one. The result again has size zero or one, and in the latter case, the function has been applied.

You have just seen how to gracefully consume an optional value when it is present. The other strategy for working with optional values is to produce an alternative if no value is present. Often, there is a default that you want to use when there was no match, perhaps the empty string:

```
String result = optionalString.orElse("");
    // The wrapped string, or "" if none
```

You can also invoke code to compute the default,

```
String result = optionalString.orElseGet(() -> System.getProperty("user.dir"));
    // The function is only called when needed
```

Or, if you want to throw another exception if there is no value,

```
String result = optionalString.orElseThrow(NoSuchElementException::new);
    // Supply a method that yields an exception object
```

2.7.2 Creating Optional Values

So far, we have discussed how to consume an Optional object that someone else created. If you write a method that creates an Optional object, there are several static methods for that purpose. Either create an Optional.of(result) or Optional.empty(). For example,

```
public static Optional<Double> inverse(Double x) {
    return x == 0 ? Optional.empty() : Optional.of(1 / x);
}
```

The ofNullable method is intended as a bridge from the use of null values to optional values. Optional.ofNullable(obj) returns Optional.of(obj) if obj is not null, and Optional.empty() otherwise.

2.7.3 Composing Optional Value Functions with flatMap

Suppose you have a method f yielding an Optional<T>, and the target type T has a method g yielding an Optional<U>. If they were normal methods, you could compose them by calling s.f().g(). But that composition doesn't work here, since s.f() has type Optional<T>, has not T. Instead, call

```
Optional<U> result = s.f().flatMap(T::g);
```

If s.f() is present, then g is applied to it. Otherwise, an empty Optional<U> is returned.

Clearly, you can repeat that process if you have more methods or lambdas that yield Optional values. You can then build a pipeline of steps that succeeds only when all parts do, simply by chaining calls to flatMap.

"build a pipeline"

For example, consider the safe inverse method of the preceding section. Suppose we also have a safe square root:

```
public static Optional<Double> squareRoot(Double x) {
    return x < 0 ? Optional.empty() : Optional.of(Math.sqrt(x));
}
```

Then you can compute the square root of the inverse as

```
Optional<Double> result = inverse(x).flatMap(MyMath::squareRoot);
```

or, if you prefer,   *good name*

```
Optional<Double> result =
    Optional.of(-4.0).flatMap(Test::inverse).flatMap(Test::squareRoot);
```

If either the inverse method or the squareRoot returns Optional.empty(), the result is empty.

NOTE: You have already seen a flatMap method in the Stream interface (see Section 2.3, "The filter, map, and flatMap Methods," on page 25). That method was used to compose two methods that yield streams, by flattening out the resulting stream of streams. The Optional.flatMap method works in the same way if you consider an optional value to be a stream of size zero or one.

2.8 Reduction Operations

If you want to compute a sum, or combine the elements of a stream to a result in another way, you can use one of the reduce methods. The simplest form takes a binary function and keeps applying it, starting with the first two elements. It's easy to explain this if the function is the sum:

```
Stream<Integer> values = ...;
Optional<Integer> sum = values.reduce((x, y) -> x + y)
```

In this case, the reduce method computes $v_0 + v_1 + v_2 + \ldots$, where the v_i are the stream elements. The method returns an Optional because there is no valid result if the stream is empty.

NOTE: In this case, you can write values.reduce(Integer::sum) instead of values.reduce((x, y) -> x + y).

In general, if the `reduce` method has a reduction operation *op*, the reduction yields $v_0\ op\ v_1\ op\ v_2\ op\ \ldots$, where we write $v_i\ op\ v_{i+1}$ for the function call $op(v_i, v_{i+1})$. The operation should be *associative*: It shouldn't matter in which order you combine the elements. In math notation, $(x\ op\ y)\ op\ z = x\ op\ (y\ op\ z)$. This allows efficient reduction with parallel streams.

There are many associative operations that might be useful in practice, such as sum and product, string concatenation, maximum and minimum, set union and intersection. An example of an operation that is not associative is subtraction. For example, $(6 - 3) - 2 \neq 6 - (3 - 2)$.

Often, there is an *identity* e such that $e\ op\ x = x$, and you can use that element as the start of the computation. For example, 0 is the identity for addition. Then call the second form of reduce:

```
Stream<Integer> values = ...;
Integer sum = values.reduce(0, (x, y) -> x + y);
    // Computes 0 + v0 + v1 + v2 + ...
```

The identity value is returned if the stream is empty, and you no longer need to deal with the `Optional` class.

Now suppose you have a stream of objects and want to form the sum of some property, such as all lengths in a stream of strings. You can't use the simple form of reduce. It requires a function `(T, T) -> T`, with the same types for the arguments and the result. But in this situation, you have two types. The stream elements have type `String`, and the accumulated result is an integer. There is a form of reduce that can deal with this situation.

First, you supply an "accumulator" function `(total, word) -> total + word.length()`. That function is called repeatedly, forming the cumulative total. But when the computation is parallelized, there will be multiple computations of this kind, and you need to combine their results. You supply a second function for that purpose. The complete call is

```
int result = words.reduce(0,
    (total, word) -> total + word.length(),
    (total1, total2) -> total1 + total2);
```

NOTE: In practice, you probably won't use the `reduce` method a lot. It is usually easier to map to a stream of numbers and use one of its methods to compute sum, max, or min. (We discuss streams of numbers in Section 2.12, "Primitive Type Streams," on page 39.) In this particular example, you could have called `words.mapToInt(String::length).sum()`, which is both simpler and more efficient, since it doesn't involve boxing.

2.9 Collecting Results

When you are done with a stream, you often just want to look at the results in-stead of reducing them to a value. You can call the iterator method, which yields an old-fashioned iterator that you can use to visit the elements. Or you can call toArray and get an array of the stream elements.

Since it is not possible to create a generic array at runtime, the expression stream.toArray() returns an Object[] array. If you want an array of the correct type, pass in the array constructor:

```
String[] result = words.toArray(String[]::new);
  // words.toArray() has type Object[]
```

Now suppose you want to collect the results in a HashSet. If the collection is paral-lelized, you can't put the elements directly into a single HashSet because a HashSet object is not threadsafe. For that reason, you can't use reduce. Each segment needs to start out with its own empty hash set, and reduce only lets you supply one identity value. Instead, use collect. It takes three arguments:

1. A *supplier* to make new instances of the target object, for example, a constructor for a hash set

2. An *accumulator* that adds an element to the target, for example, an add method

3. A *combiner* that merges two objects into one, such as addAll

---

 NOTE: The target object need not be a collection. It could be a StringBuilder or an object that tracks a count and a sum.

Here is how the collect method works for a hash set:

```
HashSet<String> result = stream.collect(HashSet::new, HashSet::add, HashSet::addAll);
```

In practice, you don't have to do that because there is a convenient Collector inter-face for these three functions, and a Collectors class with factory methods for common collectors. To collect a stream into a list or set, you can simply call

```
List<String> result = stream.collect(Collectors.toList());
```

or

```
Set<String> result = stream.collect(Collectors.toSet());
```

If you want to control which kind of set you get, use the following call instead:

```
TreeSet<String> result = stream.collect(Collectors.toCollection(TreeSet::new));
```

Suppose you want to collect all strings in a stream by concatenating them. You can call

```
String result = stream.collect(Collectors.joining());
```

If you want a delimiter between elements, pass it to the joining method:

```
String result = stream.collect(Collectors.joining(", "));
```

If your stream contains objects other than strings, you need to first convert them to strings, like this:

```
String result = stream.map(Object::toString).collect(Collectors.joining(", "));
```

If you want to reduce the stream results to a sum, average, maximum, or minimum, then use one of the methods summarizing(Int|Long|Double). These methods take a function that maps the stream objects to a number and yield a result of type (Int|Long|Double)SummaryStatistics, with methods for obtaining the sum, average, maximum, and minumum.

```
IntSummaryStatistics summary = words.collect(
   Collectors.summarizingInt(String::length));
double averageWordLength = summary.getAverage();
double maxWordLength = summary.getMax();
```

> NOTE: So far, you have seen how to reduce or collect stream values. But perhaps you just want to print them or put them in a database. Then you can use the forEach method:
>
> ```
> stream.forEach(System.out::println);
> ```
>
> The function that you pass is applied to each element. On a parallel stream, it's your responsibility to ensure that the function can be executed concurrently. We discuss this in Section 2.13, "Parallel Streams," on page 40.
>
> On a parallel stream, the elements can be traversed in arbitrary order. If you want to execute them in stream order, call forEachOrdered instead. Of course, you might then give up most or all of the benefits of parallelism.
>
> The forEach and forEachOrdered methods are terminal operations. You cannot use the stream again after calling them. If you want to continue using the stream, use peek instead—see Section 2.4, "Extracting Substreams and Combining Streams," on page 26.

2.10 Collecting into Maps

Suppose you have a Stream<Person> and want to collect the elements into a map so that you can later look up people by their ID. The Collectors.toMap method has two function arguments that produce the map keys and values. For example,

```
Map<Integer, String> idToName = people.collect(
    Collectors.toMap(Person::getId, Person::getName));
```

In the common case that the values should be the actual elements, use `Function.identity()` for the second function.

```
Map<Integer, Person> idToPerson = people.collect(
    Collectors.toMap(Person::getId, Function.identity()));
```

If there is more than one element with the same key, the collector will throw an `IllegalStateException`. You can override that behavior by supplying a third function argument that determines the value for the key, given the existing and the new value. Your function could return the existing value, the new value, or a combination of them.

Here, we construct a map that contains, for each language in the available locales, as key its name in your default locale (such as "German"), and as value its localized name (such as "Deutsch").

```
Stream<Locale> locales = Stream.of(Locale.getAvailableLocales());
Map<String, String> languageNames = locales.collect(
    Collectors.toMap(
        l -> l.getDisplayLanguage(),
        l -> l.getDisplayLanguage(l),
        (existingValue, newValue) -> existingValue));
```

We don't care that the same language might occur twice—for example, German in Germany and in Switzerland, and we just keep the first entry.

However, suppose we want to know all languages in a given country. Then we need a `Map<String, Set<String>>`. For example, the value for "Switzerland" is the set [French, German, Italian]. At first, we store a singleton set for each language. Whenever a new language is found for a given country, we form the union of the existing and the new set.

```
Map<String, Set<String>> countryLanguageSets = locales.collect(
    Collectors.toMap(
        l -> l.getDisplayCountry(),
        l -> Collections.singleton(l.getDisplayLanguage()),
        (a, b) -> { // Union of a and b
            Set<String> r = new HashSet<>(a);
            r.addAll(b);
            return r; }));
```

You will see a simpler way of obtaining this map in the next section.

If you want a `TreeMap`, then you supply the constructor as the fourth argument. You must provide a merge function. Here is one of the examples from the beginning of the section, now yielding a `TreeMap`:

```
Map<Integer, Person> idToPerson = people.collect(
    Collectors.toMap(
        Person::getId,
        Function.identity(),
        (existingValue, newValue) -> { throw new IllegalStateException(); },
        TreeMap::new));
```

 NOTE: For each of the toMap methods, there is an equivalent toConcurrentMap method that yields a concurrent map. A single concurrent map is used in the parallel collection process. When used with a parallel stream, a shared map is more efficient than merging maps, but of course, you give up ordering.

2.11 Grouping and Partitioning

In the preceding section, you saw how to collect all languages in a given country. But the process was a bit tedious. You had to generate a singleton set for each map value, and then specify how to merge the existing and new values. Forming groups of values with the same characteristic is very common, and the groupingBy method supports it directly.

Let's look at the problem of grouping locales by country. First form this map:

```
Map<String, List<Locale>> countryToLocales = locales.collect(
    Collectors.groupingBy(Locale::getCountry));
```

The function Locale::getCountry is the *classifier function* of the grouping. You can now look up all locales for a given country code, for example

```
List<Locale> swissLocales = countryToLocales.get("CH");
    // Yields locales [it_CH, de_CH, fr_CH]
```

 NOTE: A quick refresher on locales: Each locale has a language code (such as en for English) and a country code (such as US for the United States). The locale en_US describes English in the United States, and en_IE is English in Ireland. Some countries have multiple locales. For example, ga_IE is Gaelic in Ireland, and, as the preceding example shows, my JVM knows three locales in Switzerland.

When the classifier function is a predicate function (that is, a function returning a boolean value), the stream elements are partitioned into two lists: those where the function returns true and the complement. In this case, it is more efficient to use partitioningBy instead of groupingBy. For example, here we split all locales into those that use English, and all others:

```
Map<Boolean, List<Locale>> englishAndOtherLocales = locales.collect(
   Collectors.partitioningBy(l -> l.getLanguage().equals("en")));
List<Locale>> englishLocales = englishAndOtherLocales.get(true);
```

> NOTE: If you call the groupingByConcurrent method, you get a concurrent map
> that, when used with a parallel stream, is concurrently populated. This is
> entirely analogous to the toConcurrentMap method.

The groupingBy method yields a map whose values are lists. If you want to process those lists in some way, you supply a "downstream collector." For example, if you want sets instead of lists, you can use the Collectors.toSet collector that you saw in the preceding section:

```
Map<String, Set<Locale>> countryToLocaleSet = locales.collect(
   groupingBy(Locale::getCountry, toSet()));
```

> NOTE: In this example, as well as the remaining examples of this chapter,
> I assume a static import of java.util.stream.Collectors.* to make the
> expressions easier to read.

Several other collectors are provided for downstream processing of grouped elements:

- counting produces a count of the collected elements. For example,

  ```
  Map<String, Long> countryToLocaleCounts = locales.collect(
     groupingBy(Locale::getCountry, counting()));
  ```

  counts how many locales there are for each country.

- summing(Int | Long | Double) takes a function argument, applies the function to the downstream elements, and produces their sum. For example,

  ```
  Map<String, Integer> stateToCityPopulation = cities.collect(
     groupingBy(City::getState, summingInt(City::getPopulation)));
  ```

  computes the sum of populations per state in a stream of cities.

- maxBy and minBy take a comparator and produce maximum and minimum of the downstream elements. For example,

  ```
  Map<String, City> stateToLargestCity = cities.collect(
     groupingBy(City::getState,
        maxBy(Comparator.comparing(City::getPopulation))));
  ```

  produces the largest city per state.

- `mapping` applies a function to downstream results, and it requires yet another collector for processing its results. For example,

```
Map<String, Optional<String>> stateToLongestCityName = cities.collect(
    groupingBy(City::getState,
        mapping(City::getName,
            maxBy(Comparator.comparing(String::length)))));
```

Here, we group cities by state. Within each state, we produce the names of the cities and reduce by maximum length.

The `mapping` method also yields a nicer solution to a problem from the preceding section, to gather a set of all languages in a country.

```
Map<String, Set<String>> countryToLanguages = locales.collect(
    groupingBy(l -> l.getDisplayCountry(),
        mapping(l -> l.getDisplayLanguage(),
            toSet())));
```

In the preceding section, I used `toMap` instead of `groupingBy`. In this form, you don't need to worry about combining the individual sets.

- If the grouping or mapping function has return type `int`, `long`, or `double`, you can collect elements into a summary statistics object, as discussed in Section 2.9, "Collecting Results," on page 33. For example,

```
Map<String, IntSummaryStatistics> stateToCityPopulationSummary = cities.collect(
    groupingBy(City::getState,
        summarizingInt(City::getPopulation)));
```

Then you can get the sum, count, average, minimum, and maximum of the function values from the summary statistics objects of each group.

- Finally, the `reducing` methods apply a general reduction to downstream elements. There are three forms: `reducing(binaryOperator)`, `reducing(identity, binaryOperator)`, and `reducing(identity, mapper, binaryOperator)`. In the first form, the identity is `null`. (Note that this is different from the forms of `Stream::reduce`, where the method without an identity parameter yields an `Optional` result.) In the third form, the `mapper` function is applied and its values are reduced.

Here is an example that gets a comma-separated string of all city names in each state. We map each city to its name and then concatenate them.

```
Map<String, String> stateToCityNames = cities.collect(
    groupingBy(City::getState,
        reducing("", City::getName,
            (s, t) -> s.length() == 0 ? t : s + ", " + t)));
```

As with `Stream.reduce`, `Collectors.reducing` is rarely necessary. In this case, you can achieve the same result more naturally as

```
Map<String, String> stateToCityNames = cities.collect(
    groupingBy(City::getState,
        mapping(City::getName,
            joining(", "))));
```

Frankly, the downstream collectors can yield very convoluted expressions. You should only use them in connection with groupingBy or partitioningBy to process the "downstream" map values. Otherwise, simply apply methods such as map, reduce, count, max, or min directly on streams.

2.12 Primitive Type Streams

So far, we have collected integers in a Stream<Integer>, even though it is clearly inefficient to wrap each integer into a wrapper object. The same is true for the other primitive types double, float, long, short, char, byte, and boolean. The stream library has specialized types IntStream, LongStream, and DoubleStream that store primitive values directly, without using wrappers. If you want to store short, char, byte, and boolean, use an IntStream, and for float, use a DoubleStream. The library designers didn't think it was worth adding another five stream types.

To create an IntStream, you can call the IntStream.of and Arrays.stream methods:

```
IntStream stream = IntStream.of(1, 1, 2, 3, 5);
stream = Arrays.stream(values, from, to); // values is an int[] array
```

As with object streams, you can also use the static generate and iterate methods. In addition, IntStream and LongStream have static methods range and rangeClosed that generate integer ranges with step size one:

```
IntStream zeroToNinetyNine = IntStream.range(0, 100); // Upper bound is excluded
IntStream zeroToHundred = IntStream.rangeClosed(0, 100); // Upper bound is included
```

The CharSequence interface has methods codePoints and chars that yield an IntStream of the Unicode codes of the characters or of the code units in the UTF-16 encoding. (If you don't know what code units are, you probably shouldn't use the chars method. Read up on the sordid details in *Core Java, 9th Edition, Volume 1*, Section 3.3.3.)

```
String sentence = "\uD835\uDD46 is the set of octonions.";
    // \uD835\uDD46 is the UTF-16 encoding of the letter 𝕆, unicode U+1D546

IntStream codes = sentence.codePoints();
    // The stream with hex values 1D546 20 69 73 20 ...
```

When you have a stream of objects, you can transform it to a primitive type stream with the mapToInt, mapToLong, or mapToDouble methods. For example, if you have a stream of strings and want to process their lengths as integers, you might as well do it in an IntStream:

```
Stream<String> words = ...;
IntStream lengths = words.mapToInt(String::length);
```

To convert a primitive type stream to an object stream, use the boxed method:

```
Stream<Integer> integers = IntStream.range(0, 100).boxed();
```

Generally, the methods on primitive type streams are analogous to those on object streams. Here are the most notable differences:

- The toArray methods return primitive type arrays.

- Methods that yield an optional result return an OptionalInt, OptionalLong, or OptionalDouble. These classes are analogous to the Optional class, but they have methods getAsInt, getAsLong, and getAsDouble instead of the get method.

- There are methods sum, average, max, and min that return the sum, average, maximum, and minimum. These methods are not defined for object streams.

- The summaryStatistics method yields an object of type IntSummaryStatistics, LongSummaryStatistics, or DoubleSummaryStatistics that can simultaneously report the sum, average, maximum, and minimum of the stream.

> NOTE: The Random class has methods ints, longs, and doubles that return primitive type streams of random numbers.

2.13 Parallel Streams

Streams make it easy to parallelize bulk operations. The process is mostly automatic, but you need to follow a few rules. First of all, you must have a parallel stream. By default, stream operations create sequential streams, except for Collection.parallelStream(). The parallel method converts any sequential stream into a parallel one. For example:

```
Stream<String> parallelWords = Stream.of(wordArray).parallel();
```

As long as the stream is in parallel mode when the terminal method executes, all lazy intermediate stream operations will be parallelized.

When stream operations run in parallel, the intent is that the same result is returned as if they had run serially. It is important that the operations are *stateless* and can be executed in an arbitrary order.

Here is an example of something you cannot do. Suppose you want to count all short words in a stream of strings:

```
int[] shortWords = new int[12];
words.parallel().forEach(
   s -> { if (s.length() < 12) shortWords[s.length()]++; });
      // Error—race condition!
System.out.println(Arrays.toString(shortWords));
```

[handwritten margin notes: "next", "index for doubles as value element is count"]

This is very, very bad code. The function passed to forEach runs concurrently in multiple threads, updating a shared array. That's a classic race condition. If you run this program multiple times, you are quite likely to get a different sequence of counts in each run, each of them wrong.

It is your responsibility to ensure that any functions that you pass to parallel stream operations are threadsafe. In our example, you could use an array of AtomicInteger objects for the counters (see Exercise 12). Or you could simply use the facilities of the streams library and group strings by length (see Exercise 13).

By default, streams that arise from ordered collections (arrays and lists), from ranges, generators, and iterators, or from calling Stream.sorted, are *ordered*. Results are accumulated in the order of the original elements, and are entirely predictable. If you run the same operations twice, you will get exactly the same results.

Ordering does not preclude parallelization. For example, when computing stream.map(fun), the stream can be partitioned into *n* segments, each of which is concurrently processed. Then the results are reassembled in order.

Some operations can be more effectively parallelized when the ordering requirement is dropped. By calling the Stream.unordered method, you indicate that you are not interested in ordering. One operation that can benefit from this is Stream.distinct. On an ordered stream, distinct retains the first of all equal elements. That impedes parallelization—the thread processing a segment can't know which elements to discard until the preceding segment has been processed. If it is acceptable to retain *any* of the unique elements, all segments can be processed concurrently (using a shared set to track duplicates).

You can also speed up the limit method by dropping ordering. If you just want any n elements from a stream and you don't care which ones you get, call

```
Stream<T> sample = stream.parallel().unordered().limit(n);
```

As discussed in Section 2.10, "Collecting into Maps," on page 34, merging maps is expensive. For that reason, the Collectors.groupingByConcurrent method uses a shared concurrent map. Clearly, to benefit from parallelism, the order of the map values will not be the same as the stream order. Even on an ordered stream, that collector has a "characteristic" of being unordered, so that it can be used efficiently without having to make the stream unordered. You still need to make the stream parallel, though:

```
Map<String, List<String>> result = cities.parallel().collect(
    Collectors.groupingByConcurrent(City::getState));
    // Values aren't collected in stream order
```

> CAUTION: It is very important that you don't modify the collection that is backing a stream while carrying out a stream operation (even if the modification is threadsafe). Remember that streams don't collect their own data—the data is always in a separate collection. If you were to modify that collection, the outcome of the stream operations would be undefined. The JDK documentation refers to this requirement as *noninterference*. It applies both to sequential and parallel streams.
>
> To be exact, since intermediate stream operations are lazy, it is possible to mutate the collection up to the point when the terminal operation executes. For example, the following is correct:
>
> ```
> List<String> wordList = ...;
> Stream<String> words = wordList.stream();
> wordList.add("END"); // Ok
> long n = words.distinct().count();
> ```
>
> But this code is not:
>
> ```
> Stream<String> words = wordList.stream();
> words.forEach(s -> if (s.length() < 12) wordList.remove(s));
>     // Error—interference
> ```

interference

2.14 Functional Interfaces

In this chapter, you have seen many operations whose argument is a function. For example, the `Streams.filter` method takes a function argument:

```
Stream<String> longWords = words.filter(s -> s.length() >= 12);
```

In the javadoc of the `Stream` class, the `filter` method is declared as follows:

```
Stream<T> filter(Predicate<? super T> predicate)
```

To understand the documentation, you have to know what a `Predicate` is. It is an interface with one nondefault method returning a `boolean` value:

```
public interface Predicate<T> {
    boolean test(T argument);
}
```

In practice, one usually passes a lambda expression or method reference, so the name of the method doesn't really matter. The important part is the `boolean` return type. When reading the documentation of Stream.filter, just remember that a Predicate is a function returning a boolean.

 NOTE: When you look closely at the declaration of Stream.filter, you will note the wildcard type Predicate<? super T>. This is common for function parameters. For example, suppose Employee is a subclass of Person, and you have a Stream<Employee>. You can filter the stream (where T is Employee) with a Predicate<Employee>, a Predicate<Person>, or a Predicate<Object>. This flexibility is particularly important for supplying method references. For example, you may want to use Person::isAlive to filter a Stream<Employee>. That only works because of the wildcard in the parameter of the filter method.

Table 2–1 summarizes the functional interfaces that occur as parameters of the Stream and Collectors methods. You will see additional functional interfaces in the next chapter.

Table 2–1 Functional Interfaces Used in the Stream API

Functional Interface	Parameter Types	Return Type	Description
Supplier<T>	None	T	Supplies a value of type T
Consumer<T>	T	void	Consumes a value of type T
BiConsumer<T, U>	T, U	void	Consumes values of types T and U
Predicate<T>	T	boolean	A Boolean-valued function
ToIntFunction<T> ToLongFunction<T> ToDoubleFunction<T>	T	int long double	An int-, long-, or double-valued function
IntFunction<R> LongFunction<R> DoubleFunction<R>	int long double	R	A function with argument of type int, long, or double
Function<T, R>	T	R	A function with argument of type T
BiFunction<T, U, R>	T, U	R	A function with arguments of types T and U
UnaryOperator<T>	T	T	A unary operator on the type T
BinaryOperator<T>	T, T	T	A binary operator on the type T

Exercises

1. Write a parallel version of the for loop in Section 2.1, "From Iteration to Stream Operations," on page 22. Obtain the number of processors. Make that many separate threads, each working on a segment of the list, and total up the results as they come in. (You don't want the threads to update a single counter. Why?)

2. Verify that asking for the first five long words does not call the filter method once the fifth long word has been found. Simply log each method call.

3. Measure the difference when counting long words with a parallelStream instead of a stream. Call System.nanoTime before and after the call, and print the difference. Switch to a larger document (such as *War and Peace*) if you have a fast computer.

4. Suppose you have an array int[] values = { 1, 4, 9, 16 }. What is Stream.of(values)? How do you get a stream of int instead?

5. Using Stream.iterate, make an infinite stream of random numbers—not by calling Math.random but by directly implementing a *linear congruential generator*. In such a generator, you start with $x_0 = seed$ and then produce $x_{n + 1} = (a\, x_n + c)\, \% \, m$, for appropriate values of a, c, and m. You should implement a method with parameters a, c, m, and seed that yields a Stream<Long>. Try out $a = 25214903917$, $c = 11$, and $m = 2^{48}$.

6. The characterStream method in Section 2.3, "The filter, map, and flatMap Methods," on page 25, was a bit clumsy, first filling an array list and then turning it into a stream. Write a stream-based one-liner instead. One approach is to make a stream of integers from 0 to s.length() - 1 and map that with the s::charAt method reference.

7. Your manager asks you to write a method public static <T> boolean isFinite(Stream<T> stream). Why isn't that such a good idea? Go ahead and write it anyway.

8. Write a method public static <T> Stream<T> zip(Stream<T> first, Stream<T> second) that alternates elements from the streams first and second, stopping when one of them runs out of elements.

9. Join all elements in a Stream<ArrayList<T>> to one ArrayList<T>. Show how to do this with the three forms of reduce.

10. Write a call to reduce that can be used to compute the average of a Stream<Double>. Why can't you simply compute the sum and divide by count()?

11. It should be possible to concurrently collect stream results in a single ArrayList, instead of merging multiple array lists, provided it has been constructed with

the stream's size, since concurrent set operations at disjoint positions are threadsafe. How can you achieve that?

12. Count all short words in a parallel `Stream<String>`, as described in Section 2.13, "Parallel Streams," on page 40, by updating an array of `AtomicInteger`. Use the atomic `getAndIncrement` method to safely increment each counter.

13. Repeat the preceding exercise, but filter out the short strings and use the `collect` method with `Collectors.groupingBy` and `Collectors.counting`.

Programming with Lambdas

Chapter 3

In the first two chapters, you saw the basic syntax and semantics of lambda expressions as well as the stream API that makes extensive use of them. In this chapter, you will learn how to create your own libraries that make use of lambda expressions and functional interfaces.

The key points of this chapter are:

- The main reason for using a lambda expression is to defer the execution of the code until an appropriate time.

- When a lambda expression is executed, make sure to provide any required data as inputs.

- Choose one of the existing functional interfaces if you can.

- It is often useful to write methods that return an instance of a functional interface.

- When you work with transformations, consider how you can compose them.

- To compose transformations lazily, you need to keep a list of all pending transformations and apply them in the end.

- If you need to apply a lambda many times, you often have a chance to split up the work into subtasks that execute concurrently.

- Think what should happen when you work with a lambda expression that throws an exception.

- When working with generic functional interfaces, use ? super wildcards for argument types, ? extends wildcards for return types.
- When working with generic types that can be transformed by functions, consider supplying map and flatMap.

3.1 Deferred Execution

The point of all lambdas is *deferred execution*. After all, if you wanted to execute some code right now, you'd do that, without wrapping it inside a lambda. There are many reasons for executing code later, such as

- Running the code in a separate thread
- Running the code multiple times
- Running the code at the right point in an algorithm (for example, the comparison operation in sorting)
- Running the code when something happens (a button was clicked, data has arrived, and so on)
- Running the code only when necessary

It is a good idea to think through what you want to achieve when you set out programming with lambdas.

Let us look at a simple example. Suppose you log an event:

```
logger.info("x: " + x + ", y: " + y);
```

What happens if the log level is set to suppress INFO messages? The message string is computed and passed to the info method, which then decides to throw it away. Wouldn't it be nicer if the string concatenation only happened when necessary?

Running code only when necessary is a use case for lambdas. The standard idiom is to wrap the code in a no-arg lambda:

```
() -> "x: " + x + ", y: " + y
```

Now we need to write a method that

1. Accepts the lambda
2. Checks whether it should be called
3. Calls it when necessary

To accept the lambda, we need to pick (or, in rare cases, provide) a functional interface. We discuss the process of choosing an interface in more detail in Section 3.3, "Choosing a Functional Interface," on page 50. Here, a good choice is a Supplier<String>. The following method provides lazy logging:

```
public static void info(Logger logger, Supplier<String> message) {
    if (logger.isLoggable(Level.INFO))
        logger.info(message.get());
}
```

We use the isLoggable method of the Logger class to decide whether INFO messages should be logged. If so, we invoke the lambda by calling its abstract method, which happens to be called get.

 NOTE: Deferring logging messages is such a good idea that the Java 8 library designers beat me to it. The info method, as well as the other logging methods, now have variants that accept a Supplier<String>. You can directly call logger.info(() -> "x: " + x + ", y:" + y). However, see Exercise 1 for a potentially useful refinement.

3.2 Parameters of Lambda Expressions

When you ask your user to supply a comparator, it is pretty obvious that the comparator has two arguments—the values to be compared.

```
Arrays.sort(names,
    (s, t) -> Integer.compare(s.length(), t.length())); // Compare strings s and t
```

Now consider a different example. This method repeats an action multiple times:

```
public static void repeat(int n, IntConsumer action) {
    for (int i = 0; i < n; i++) action.accept(i);
}
```

Why an IntConsumer and not a Runnable? We tell the action in which iteration it occurs, which might be useful information. The action needs to capture that input in a parameter

```
repeat(10, i -> System.out.println("Countdown: " + (9 - i)));
```

Another example is an event handler

```
button.setOnAction(event -> action);
```

The event object carries information that the action may need.

In general, you want to design your algorithm so that it passes any required information as arguments. For example, when editing an image, it makes sense to have the user supply a function that computes the color for a pixel. Such a function might need to know not just the current color, but also where the pixel is in the image, or what the neighboring pixels are.

However, if these arguments are rarely needed, consider supplying a second version that doesn't force users into accepting unwanted arguments:

```
public static void repeat(int n, Runnable action) {
    for (int i = 0; i < n; i++) action.run();
}
```

This version can be called as

```
repeat(10, () -> System.out.println("Hello, World!"));
```

3.3 Choosing a Functional Interface

In most functional programming languages, function types are *structural*. To specify a function that maps two strings to an integer, you use a type that looks something like Function2<String, String, Integer> or (String, String) -> int. In Java, you instead declare the intent of the function, using a functional interface such as Comparator<String>. In the theory of programming languages this is called *nominal* typing.

Of course, there are many situations where you want to accept "any function" without particular semantics. There are a number of generic function types for that purpose (see Table 3–1), and it's a very good idea to use one of them when you can.

For example, suppose you write a method to process files that match a certain criterion. Should you use the descriptive java.io.FileFilter class or a Predicate<File>? I strongly recommend that you use the standard Predicate<File>. The only reason not to do so would be if you already have many useful methods producing FileFilter instances.

 NOTE: Most of the standard functional interfaces have nonabstract methods for producing or combining functions. For example, Predicate.isEqual(a) is the same as a::equals, provided a is not null. And there are default methods and, or, negate for combining predicates. For example, Predicate.isEqual(a).or(Predicate.isEqual(b)) is the same as x -> a.equals(x) || b.equals(x).

Consider another example. We want to transform images, applying a Color -> Color function to each pixel. For example, the brightened image in Figure 3–1 is obtained by calling

```
Image brightenedImage = transform(image, Color::brighter);
```

Table 3–1 Common Functional Interfaces

Functional Interface	Parameter Types	Return Type	Abstract Method Name	Description	Other Methods
Runnable	none	void	run	Runs an action without arguments or return value	
Supplier<T>	none	T	get	Supplies a value of type T	
Consumer<T>	T	void	accept	Consumes a value of type T	andThen
BiConsumer<T, U>	T, U	void	accept	Consumes values of types T and U	andThen
Function<T, R>	T	R	apply	A function with argument of type T	compose, andThen, identity
BiFunction<T, U, R>	T, U	R	apply	A function with arguments of types T and U	andThen
UnaryOperator<T> Function<T,T>	T	T	apply	A unary operator on the type T	compose, andThen, identity
BinaryOperator<T>	T, T	T	apply	A binary operator on the type T	andThen, maxBy, minBy
Predicate<T>	T	boolean	test	A Boolean-valued function	and, or, negate, isEqual
BiPredicate<T, U>	T, U	boolean	test	A Boolean-valued function with two arguments	and, or, negate

Figure 3–1   The original and transformed image

There is a standard functional interface for this purpose: UnaryOperator<Color>. That is a good choice, and there is no need to come up with a ColorTransformer interface.

Here is the implementation of the transform method. Note the call to the apply method.

```
public static Image transform(Image in, UnaryOperator<Color> f) {
    int width = (int) in.getWidth();
    int height = (int) in.getHeight();
    WritableImage out = new WritableImage(width, height);
    for (int x = 0; x < width; x++)
        for (int y = 0; y < height; y++)
            out.getPixelWriter().setColor(x, y,
                f.apply(in.getPixelReader().getColor(x, y)));
    return out;
}
```

 NOTE: This method uses the Color and Image classes from JavaFX, not from java.awt. See Chapter 4 for more information on JavaFX.

Table 3–2 lists the 34 available specializations for primitive types int, long, and double. Use the specializations when you can to reduce autoboxing.

Sometimes, you need to supply your own functional interface because there is nothing in the standard library that works for you. Suppose you want to modify colors in an image, allowing users to specify a function (int, int, Color) -> Color that computes a new color depending on the (x, y) location in the image. In that case, you can define your own interface:

Table 3–2 Functional Interfaces for Primitive Types: p, q is int, long, double; P, Q is Int, Long, Double

Functional Interface	Parameter Types	Return Type	Abstract Method Name
BooleanSupplier	none	boolean	getAsBoolean
PSupplier	none	p	getAsP
PConsumer	p	void	accept
ObjPConsumer<T>	T, p	void	accept
PFunction<T>	p	T	apply
PToQFunction	p	q	applyAsQ
ToPFunction<T>	T	p	applyAsP
ToPBiFunction<T, U>	T, U	p	applyAsP
PUnaryOperator	p	p	applyAsP
PBinaryOperator	p, p	p	applyAsP
PPredicate	p	boolean	test

```
@FunctionalInterface
public interface ColorTransformer {
    Color apply(int x, int y, Color colorAtXY);
}
```

 NOTE: I called the abstract method apply because that is used for the majority of standard functional interfaces. Should you call the method process or transform or getColor instead? It doesn't matter much to users of the color manipulation code—they will usually supply a lambda expression. Sticking with the standard name simplifies the life of the implementor.

3.4 Returning Functions

In a functional programming language, functions are first-class citizens. Just like you can pass numbers to methods and have methods that produce numbers, you can have arguments and return values that are functions. This sounds abstract, but it is very useful in practice. Java is not quite a functional language because it uses functional interfaces, but the principle is the same. You have seen many

Practice

methods that accept functional interfaces. In this section, we consider methods whose return type is a functional interface.

Consider again image transformations. If you call

```
Image brightenedImage = transform(image, Color::brighter);
```

the image is brightened by a fixed amount. What if you want it even brighter, or not quite so bright? Could you supply the desired brightness as an additional parameter to transform?

```
Image brightenedImage = transform(image,
    (c, factor) -> c.deriveColor(0, 1, factor, 1), // Brighten c by factor
    1.2); // Use a factor of 1.2
```

One would have to overload transform:

```
public static <T> Image transform(Image in, BiFunction<Color, T, Color> f, T arg)
```

That can be made to work (see Exercise 6), but what if one wants to supply two arguments? Or three? There is another way. We can make a method that returns the appropriate UnaryOperator<Color>, with the brightness set:

```
public static UnaryOperator<Color> brighten(double factor) {
    return c -> c.deriveColor(0, 1, factor, 1);
}
```

 returns a function
It's a function factory

Then we can call

```
Image brightenedImage = transform(image, brighten(1.2));
```

The brighten method returns a function (or, technically, an instance of a functional interface). That function can be passed to another method (here, transform) that expects such an interface.

In general, don't be shy to write methods that produce functions. This is useful to customize the functions that you pass to methods with functional interfaces. For example, consider the Arrays.sort method with a Comparator argument. There are many ways of comparing values, and you can write a method that yields a comparator for your needs—see Exercise 7. Then you can call Arrays.sort(values, comparatorGenerator(*customization arguments*)).

> ■ NOTE: As you will see in Chapter 8, the Comparator class has several methods that yield or modify comparators.

3.5 Composition

A single-argument function transforms one value into another. If you have two such transformations, then doing one after the other is also a transformation.

Figure 3–2 First, the image is brightened, and then grayscale is applied.

Consider image manipulation: Let's first brighten an image, then turn it to grayscale (see Figure 3–2).

 NOTE: In the printed book, everything is in grayscale. Just run the program in the companion code to see the effect.

That is easy to do with our transform method:

```
Image image = new Image("eiffel-tower.jpg");
Image image2 = transform(image, Color::brighter);
Image finalImage = transform(image2, Color::grayscale);
```

But this is not very efficient. We need to make an intermediate image. For large images, that requires a considerable amount of storage. If we could compose the image operations and then apply the composite operation to each pixel, that would be better.

In this case, the image operations are instances of UnaryOperator<Color>. That type has a method compose that, for rather depressing reasons that are explored in Exercise 10, is not useful for us. But it is easy to roll our own:

```
public static <T> UnaryOperator<T> compose(UnaryOperator<T> op1,
      UnaryOperator<T> op2) {
   return t -> op2.apply(op1.apply(t));
}
```

Now we can call

```
Image finalImage = transform(image, compose(Color::brighter, Color::grayscale));
```

That is much better. Now the composed transformation is directly applied to each pixel, and there is no need for an intermediate image.

Generally, when you build a library where users can carry out one effect after another, it is a good idea to give library users the ability to compose these effects. See Exercise 11 for another example.

3.6 Laziness

In the preceding section, you saw how users of an image transformation method can precompose operations to avoid intermediate images. But why should they have to do that? Another approach is for the library to accumulate all operations and then fuse them. This is, of course, what the stream library does.

If you do lazy processing, your API needs to distinguish between intermediate operations, which accumulate the tasks to be done, and terminal operations which deliver the result. In the image processing example, we can make transform lazy, but then it needs to return another object that is not an Image. For example,

```
LatentImage latent = transform(image, Color::brighter);
```

A LatentImage can simply store the original image and a sequence of image operations.

```
public class LatentImage {
   private Image in;
   private List<UnaryOperator<Color>> pendingOperations;
   ...
}
```

This class also needs a transform method:

```
LatentImage transform(UnaryOperator<Color> f) {
   pendingOperations.add(f);
   return this;
}
```

To avoid duplicate transform methods, you can follow the approach of the stream library where an initial stream() operation is required to turn a collection into a stream. Since we can't add a method to the Image class, we can provide a LatentImage constructor or a static factory method.

```
LatentImage latent = LatentImage.from(image)
    .transform(Color::brighter).transform(Color::grayscale);
```

You can only be lazy for so long. Eventually, the work needs to be done. We can provide a toImage method that applies all operations and returns the result:

```
Image finalImage = LatentImage.from(image)
    .transform(Color::brighter).transform(Color::grayscale)
    .toImage();
```

Here is the implementation of the method:

```
public Image toImage() {
    int width = (int) in.getWidth();
    int height = (int) in.getHeight();
    WritableImage out = new WritableImage(width, height);
    for (int x = 0; x < width; x++)
        for (int y = 0; y < height; y++) {
            Color c = in.getPixelReader().getColor(x, y);
            for (UnaryOperator<Color> f : pendingOperations) c = f.apply(c);
            out.getPixelWriter().setColor(x, y, c);
        }
    return out;
}
```

The minimum thing
✓ *entity that actually*
needs transforming

 CAUTION: In real life, implementing lazy operations is quite a bit harder. Usually you have a mixture of operations, and not all of them can be applied lazily. See Exercises 12 and 13.

3.7 Parallelizing Operations

When expressing operations as functional interfaces, the caller gives up control over the processing details. As long as the operations are applied so that the correct result is achieved, the caller has nothing to complain about. In particular, the library can make use of concurrency. For example, in image processing we can split the image into multiple strips and process each strip separately.

Here is a simple way of carrying out an image transformation in parallel. This code operates on Color[][] arrays instead of Image objects because the JavaFX PixelWriter is not threadsafe.

```
public static Color[][] parallelTransform(Color[][] in, UnaryOperator<Color> f) {
   int n = Runtime.getRuntime().availableProcessors();
   int height = in.length;
   int width = in[0].length;
   Color[][] out = new Color[height][width];
   try {
      ExecutorService pool = Executors.newCachedThreadPool();
      for (int i = 0; i < n; i++) {
         int fromY = i * height / n;
         int toY = (i + 1) * height / n;
         pool.submit(() -> {
               for (int x = 0; x < width; x++)
                  for (int y = fromY; y < toY; y++)
                     out[y][x] = f.apply(in[y][x]);
            });
      }
      pool.shutdown();
      pool.awaitTermination(1, TimeUnit.HOURS);
   }
   catch (InterruptedException ex) {
      ex.printStackTrace();
   }
   return out;
}
```

(handwritten annotations: arrow pointing to "int n = Runtime.getRuntime().availableProcessors();" with a star mark; "equally divides the work among n processors")

This is, of course, just a proof of concept. Supporting image operations that combine multiple pixels would be a major challenge.

In general, when you are given an object of a functional interface and you need to invoke it many times, ask yourself whether you can take advantage of concurrency.

3.8 Dealing with Exceptions

When you write a method that accepts lambdas, you need to spend some thought on handling and reporting exceptions that may occur when the lambda expression is executed.

When an exception is thrown in a lambda expression, it is propagated to the caller. There is nothing special about executing lambda expressions, of course. They are simply method calls on some object that implements a functional interface. Often it is appropriate to let the exception bubble up to the caller.

Consider, for example:

```
public static void doInOrder(Runnable first, Runnable second) {
    first.run();
    second.run();
}
```

If `first.run()` throws an exception, then the `doInOrder` method is terminated, `second` is never run, and the caller gets to deal with the exception.

But now suppose we execute the tasks asynchronously.

```
public static void doInOrderAsync(Runnable first, Runnable second) {
    Thread t = new Thread() {
        public void run() {
            first.run();
            second.run();
        }
    };
    t.start();
}
```

If `first.run()` throws an exception, the thread is terminated, and `second` is never run. However, the `doInOrderAsync` returns right away and does the work in a separate thread, so it is not possible to have the method rethrow the exception. In this situation, it is a good idea to supply a handler:

```
public static void doInOrderAsync(Runnable first, Runnable second,
        Consumer<Throwable> handler) {
    Thread t = new Thread() {
        public void run() {
            try {
                first.run();
                second.run();
            } catch (Throwable t) {
                handler.accept(t);
            }
        }
    };
    t.start();
}
```

Now suppose that `first` produces a result that is consumed by `second`. We can still use the handler.

```
public static <T> void doInOrderAsync(Supplier<T> first, Consumer<T> second,
      Consumer<Throwable> handler) {
   Thread t = new Thread() {
      public void run() {
         try {
            T result = first.get();
            second.accept(result);
         } catch (Throwable t) {
            handler.accept(t);
         }
      }
   };
   t.start();
}
```

Alternatively, we could make second a BiConsumer<T, Throwable> and have it deal with the exception from first—see Exercise 16.

It is often inconvenient that methods in functional interfaces don't allow checked exceptions. Of course, your methods can accept functional interfaces whose methods allow checked exceptions, such as Callable<T> instead of Supplier<T>. A Callable<T> has a method that is declared as T call() throws Exception. If you want an equivalent for a Consumer or a Function, you have to create it yourself.

You sometimes see suggestions to "fix" this problem with a generic wrapper, like this:

```
public static <T> Supplier<T> unchecked(Callable<T> f) {
   return () -> {
      try {
         return f.call();
      }
      catch (Exception e) {
         throw new RuntimeException(e);
      }
      catch (Throwable t) {
         throw t;
      }
   };
}
```

Then you can pass a

```
unchecked(() -> new String(Files.readAllBytes(
   Paths.get("/etc/passwd")), StandardCharsets.UTF_8))
```

to a Supplier<String>, even though the readAllBytes method throws an IOException.

That is a solution, but not a complete fix. For example, this method cannot generate a `Consumer<T>` or a `Function<T, U>`. You would need to implement a variation of `unchecked` for each functional interface.

3.9 Lambdas and Generics

Generally, lambdas work well with generic types. You have seen a number of examples where we wrote generic mechanisms, such as the `unchecked` method of the preceding section. There are just a couple of issues to keep in mind.

One of the unhappy consequences of type erasure is that you cannot construct a generic array at runtime. For example, the `toArray()` method of `Collection<T>` and `Stream<T>` cannot call `T[] result = new T[n]`. Therefore, these methods return `Object[]` arrays. In the past, the solution was to provide a second method that accepts an array. That array was either filled or used to create a new one via reflection. For example, `Collection<T>` has a method `toArray(T[] a)`. With lambdas, you have a new option, namely to pass the constructor. That is what you do with streams:

```
String[] result = words.toArray(String[]::new);
```

When you implement such a method, the constructor expression is an `IntFunction<T[]>`, since the size of the array is passed to the constructor. In your code, you call `T[] result = constr.apply(n)`.

In this regard, lambdas help you overcome a limitation of generic types. Unfortunately, in another common situation lambdas suffer from a different limitation. To understand the problem, recall the concept of type variance.

Suppose `Employee` is a subtype of `Person`. Is a `List<Employee>` a special case of a `List<Person>`? It seems that it should be. But actually, it would be unsound. Consider this code:

```
List<Employee> staff = ...;
List<Person> tenants = staff; // Not legal, but suppose it was
tenants.add(new Person("John Q. Public")); // Adds Person to staff!
```

Note that `staff` and `tenants` are references to the same list. To make this type error impossible, we must disallow the conversion from `List<Employee>` to `List<Person>`. We say that the type parameter `T` of `List<T>` is *invariant*.

If `List` was immutable, as it is in a functional programming language, then the problem would disappear, and one could have a *covariant* list. That is what is done in languages such as Scala. However, when generics were invented, Java had very few immutable generic classes, and the language designers instead embraced a different concept: use-site variance, or "wildcards."

A method can decide to accept a `List<? extends Person>` if it only reads from the list. Then you can pass either a `List<Person>` or a `List<Employee>`. Or it can accept a

List<? super Employee> if it only writes to the list. It is okay to write employees into a List<Person>, so you can pass such a list. In general, reading is covariant (subtypes are okay) and writing is contravariant (supertypes are okay). Use-site variance is just right for mutable data structures. It gives each service the choice which variance, if any, is appropriate.

However, for function types, use-site variance is a hassle. A function type is *always* contravariant in its arguments and covariant in its return value. For example, if you have a Function<Person, Employee>, you can safely pass it on to someone who needs a Function<Employee, Person>. They will only call it with employees, whereas your function can handle any person. They will expect the function to return a person, and you give them something even better.

In Java, when you declare a generic functional interface, you can't specify that function arguments are always contravariant and return types always covariant. Instead, you have to repeat it for each use. For example, look at the javadoc for Stream<T>:

```
void forEach(Consumer<? super T> action)
Stream<T> filter(Predicate<? super T> predicate)
<R> Stream<R> map(Function<? super T, ? extends R> mapper)
```

The general rule is that you use super for argument types, extends for return types. That way, you can pass a Consumer<Object> to forEach on a Stream<String>. If it is willing to consume any object, surely it can consume strings.

But the wildcards are not always there. Look at

```
T reduce(T identity, BinaryOperator<T> accumulator)
```

Since T is the argument *and* return type of BinaryOperator, the type does not vary. In effect, the contravariance and covariance cancel each other out.

As the implementor of a method that accepts lambda expressions with generic types, you simply add ? super to any argument type that is not also a return type, and ? extends to any return type that is not also an argument type.

For example, consider the doInOrderAsync method of the preceding section. Instead of

```
public static <T> void doInOrderAsync(Supplier<T> first,
    Consumer<T> second, Consumer<Throwable> handler)
```

it should be

```
public static <T> void doInOrderAsync(Supplier<? extends T> first,
    Consumer<? super T> second, Consumer<? super Throwable> handler)
```

3.10 Monadic Operations

When you work with generic types, and with functions that yield values from these types, it is useful to supply methods that let you *compose* these functions—that is, carry out one after another. In this section, you will see a design pattern for providing such compositions.

Consider a generic type G<T> with one type parameter, such as List<T> (zero or more values of type T), Optional<T> (zero or one values of type T), or Future<T> (a value of type T that will be available in the future).

Also consider a function T -> U, or a Function<T, U> object.

It often makes sense to apply this function to a G<T> (that is, a List<T>, Optional<T>, Future<T>, and so on). How this works exactly depends on the nature of the generic type G. For example, applying a function f to a List with elements $e_1, \ldots, e_n$ means creating a list with elements $f(e_1), \ldots, f(e_n)$.

Applying f to an Optional<T> containing v means creating an Optional<U> containing $f(v)$. But if f is applied to an empty Optional<T> without a value, the result is an empty Optional<U>.

Applying f to a Future<T> simply means to apply it whenever it is available. The result is a Future<U>.

By tradition, this operation is usually called map. There is a map method for Stream and Optional. The CompletableFuture class that we will discuss in Chapter 6 has an operation that does just what map should do, but it is called thenApply. There is no map for a plain Future<V>, but it is not hard to supply one (see Exercise 21).

So far, that is a fairly straightforward idea. It gets more complex when you look at functions T -> G<U> instead of functions T -> U. For example, consider getting the web page for a URL. Since it takes some time to fetch the page, that is a function URL -> Future<String>. Now suppose you have a Future<URL>, a URL that will arrive sometime. Clearly it makes sense to map the function to that Future. Wait for the URL to arrive, then feed it to the function and wait for the string to arrive. This operation has traditionally been called flatMap.

The name flatMap comes from sets. Suppose you have a "many-valued" function—a function computing a set of possible answers. And then you have another such function. How can you compose these functions? If $f(x)$ is the set $\{y_1, \ldots, y_n\}$, you apply g to each element, yielding $\{g(y_1), \ldots, g(y_n)\}$. But each of the $g(y_i)$ is a *set*. You want to "flatten" the set of sets so that you get the set of all possible values of both functions.

There is a flatMap for Optional<T> as well. Given a function T -> Optional<U>, flatMap unwraps the value in the Optional and applies the function, except if either the source or target option was not present. It does exactly what the set-based flatMap would have done on sets with size 0 or 1.

Generally, when you design a type G<T> and a function T -> U, think whether it makes sense to define a map that yields a G<U>. Then, generalize to functions T -> G<U> and, if appropriate, provide flatMap.

 NOTE: These operations are important in the theory of monads, but you don't need to know the theory to understand map and flatMap. The concept of mapping a function is both straightforward and useful, and the point of this section is to make you aware of it.

Exercises

1. Enhance the lazy logging technique by providing conditional logging. A typical call would be logIf(Level.FINEST, () -> i == 10, () -> "a[10] = " + a[10]). Don't evaluate the condition if the logger won't log the message.

2. When you use a ReentrantLock, you are required to lock and unlock with the idiom

```
myLock.lock();
try {
    some action
} finally {
    myLock.unlock();
}
```

Provide a method withLock so that one can call

```
withLock(myLock, () -> { some action })
```

3. Java 1.4 added assertions to the language, with an assert keyword. Why were assertions not supplied as a library feature? Could they be implemented as a library feature in Java 8?

4. How many functional interfaces with Filter in their name can you find in the Java API? Which ones add value over Predicate<T>?

5. Here is a concrete example of a ColorTransformer. We want to put a frame around an image, like this:

First, implement a variant of the transform method of Section 3.3, "Choosing a Functional Interface," on page 50, with a ColorTransformer instead of an UnaryOperator<Color>. Then call it with an appropriate lambda expression to put a 10 pixel gray frame replacing the pixels on the border of an image.

6. Complete the method

```
public static <T> Image transform(Image in, BiFunction<Color, T, Color> f, T arg)
```

   from Section 3.4, "Returning Functions," on page 53.

7. Write a method that generates a Comparator<String> that can be normal or reversed, case-sensitive or case-insensitive, space-sensitive or space-insensitive, or any combination thereof. Your method should return a lambda expression.

8. Generalize Exercise 5 by writing a static method that yields a ColorTransformer that adds a frame of arbitrary thickness and color to an image.

9. Write a method lexicographicComparator(String... fieldNames) that yields a comparator that compares the given fields in the given order. For example, a lexicographicComparator("lastname", "firstname") takes two objects and, using reflection, gets the values of the lastname field. If they are different, return the difference, otherwise move on to the firstname field. If all fields match, return 0.

10. Why can't one call

```
UnaryOperator op = Color::brighter;
Image finalImage = transform(image, op.compose(Color::grayscale));
```

   Look carefully at the return type of the compose method of UnaryOperator<T>. Why is it not appropriate for the transform method? What does that say about the utility of structural and nominal types when it comes to function composition?

11. Implement static methods that can compose two ColorTransformer objects, and a static method that turns a UnaryOperator<Color> into a ColorTransformer that ignores the *x*- and *y*-coordinates. Then use these methods to add a gray frame to a brightened image. (See Exercise 5 for the gray frame.)

12. Enhance the LatentImage class in Section 3.6, "Laziness," on page 56, so that it supports both UnaryOperator<Color> and ColorTransformer. Hint: Adapt the former to the latter.

13. Convolution filters such as blur or edge detection compute a pixel from neighboring pixels. To blur an image, replace each color value by the average of itself and its eight neighbors. For edge detection, replace each color value *c* with $4c - n - e - s - w$, where the other colors are those of the pixel to the north, east, south, and west. Note that these cannot be implemented lazily, using the approach of Section 3.6, "Laziness," on page 56, since they require the image from the previous stage (or at least the neighboring pixels) to have been computed. Enhance the lazy image processing to deal with these operations. Force computation of the previous stage when one of these operators is evaluated.

14. To deal with lazy evaluation on a per-pixel basis, change the transformers so that they are passed a PixelReader object from which they can read other pixels in the image. For example, (x, y, reader) -> reader.get(width - x, y) is a mirroring operation. The convolution filters from the preceding exercises can be easily implemented in terms of such a reader. The straightforward operations would simply have the form (x, y, reader) -> reader.get(x, y).grayscale(), and you can provide an adapter from UnaryOperation<Color>. A PixelReader is at a particular level in the pipeline of operations. Keep a cache of recently read pixels at each level in the pipeline. If a reader is asked for a pixel, it looks in the cache (or in the original image at level 0); if that fails, it constructs a reader that asks the previous transform.

15. Combine the lazy evaluation of Section 3.6, "Laziness," on page 56, with the parallel evaluation of Section 3.7, "Parallelizing Operations," on page 57.

16. Implement the doInOrderAsync of Section 3.8, "Dealing with Exceptions," on page 58, where the second parameter is a BiConsumer<T, Throwable>. Provide a plausible use case. Do you still need the third parameter?

17. Implement a doInParallelAsync(Runnable first, Runnable second, Consumer<Throwable>) method that executes first and second in parallel, calling the handler if either method throws an exception.

18. Implement a version of the unchecked method in Section 3.8, "Dealing with Exceptions," on page 58, that generates a Function<T, U> from a lambda that throws checked exceptions. Note that you will need to find or provide a functional interface whose abstract method throws arbitrary exceptions.

19. Look at the Stream<T> method <U> U reduce(U identity, BiFunction<U,? super T,U> accumulator, BinaryOperator<U> combiner). Should U be declared as ? super U in the first type argument to BiFunction? Why or why not?

20. Supply a static method <T, U> List<U> map(List<T>, Function<T, U>).

21. Supply a static method <T, U> Future<U> map(Future<T>, Function<T, U>). Return an object of an anonymous class that implements all methods of the Future interface. In the get methods, invoke the function.

22. Is there a flatMap operation for CompletableFuture? If so, what is it?

23. Define a map operation for a class Pair<T> that represents a pair of objects of type T.

24. Can you define a flatMap method for Pair<T>? If so, what is it? If not, why not?

JavaFX

Topics in This Chapter

Chapter

JavaFX is the recommended user interface toolkit for writing rich client applications with Java. JavaFX is now bundled with all supported versions of Oracle's Java platform. In this chapter, you will learn the basics of JavaFX development. If you develop rich client user interface platforms, you will see how to transition from Swing to JavaFX. If you don't, skim over the chapter anyway so you can understand the sample applications we use elsewhere when it is convenient to illustrate a concept with a graphical program.

The key points of this chapter are:

- A scene graph is made up of nodes which may contain other nodes.
- A scene is displayed on a stage (a top-level window, the surface of an applet, or the full screen).
- Some controls (such as buttons) emit events, but most JavaFX events come from property changes.
- JavaFX properties emit change and invalidation events.
- When you bind a property to another, it is updated when the other one changes.
- JavaFX uses layout panes that work similar to layout managers in Swing.
- You can specify layout with the FXML markup language.
- You can use CSS to change the visual appearance of your application.

- It is easy to implement animations and special effects.
- JavaFX provides some advanced controls out of the box, such as charts, an embedded WebKit browser, and a media player.

4.1 A Brief History of Java GUI Programming

When Java was born, the Internet was in its infancy and personal computers were on every desktop. Business applications were implemented with "fat clients"—programs with lots of buttons and sliders and text fields that communicated with a server. This was considered a lot nicer than the "dumb terminal" applications from an even earlier era. Java 1.0 included the AWT, a toolkit for graphical user interfaces, that had the distinction of being cross-platform. The idea was to serve up the fat clients over the nascent Web, eliminating the cost of managing and updating the applications on every desktop.

The AWT had a noble idea: provide a common programming interface for the native buttons, sliders, text fields, and so on of various operating systems. But it didn't work very well. There were subtle differences in the functionality of the user interface widgets in each operating system, and what should have been "write once, run anywhere" turned into "write many times, debug everywhere."

Next came Swing. The central idea behind Swing was not to use the native widgets, but to paint its own. That way, the user interface would look and feel the same on every platform. Or, if users preferred, they could ask for the native look and feel of their platform, and the Swing widgets would be painted to match the native ones. Of course, all that painting was slow, and users complained. After a while, computers got faster, and users complained that Swing was ugly—indeed, it had fallen behind the native widgets that had been spruced up with animations and fancy effects. More ominously, Flash was increasingly used to create user interfaces with even flashier effects that didn't use the native controls at all.

In 2007, Sun Microsystems introduced a new technology, called JavaFX, as a competitor to Flash. It ran on the Java VM but had its own programming language, called JavaFX Script. The language was optimized for programming animations and fancy effects. Programmers complained about the need to learn a new language, and they stayed away in droves. In 2011, Oracle released a new version, JavaFX 2.0, that had a Java API and no longer needed a separate programming language. As of Java 7 update 6, JavaFX 2.2 has been bundled with the JDK and JRE. Since it wouldn't be a true part of Java if it didn't have crazy jumps in version numbers, the version accompanying Java 8 is called JavaFX 8.

Of course, Flash is now a bad memory, and most user interfaces live in a browser or a mobile device. Still, there are situations where a "fat client" on a desktop makes users more productive. Also, Java now runs on ARM processors, and there are embedded systems that need user interfaces, such as kiosks and in-car displays. JavaFX is what Oracle wants us to use for those applications. Why didn't Oracle just put the good parts of JavaFX into Swing? Swing would have to be redesigned from the ground up to run efficiently on modern graphics hardware. Oracle decided that it wasn't worth the trouble and declared that Swing will not be further developed.

In this chapter, we go over the basics of writing user interfaces in JavaFX, focusing on boring business applications with buttons, sliders, and text fields, not the flashy effects that were the original motivation behind JavaFX.

4.2 Hello, JavaFX!

Let's start with a simple program that shows a message (see Figure 4–1). Like in Swing, use a *label*:

```
Label message = new Label("Hello, JavaFX!");
```

 NOTE: There are no unsightly J prefixes. In Swing, the equivalent control was called JLabel to distinguish it from the AWT Label.

We increase the font size:

```
message.setFont(new Font(100));
```

This Font constructor makes a font object representing the default font at 100 points.

In JavaFX, you put everything you want to show onto a *scene*. There, you can decorate and animate your "actors"—that is, your controls and shapes. In our program, we won't do any decorating or animating, but we still need the scene. And the scene must reside in a *stage*. That is a top-level window if the program runs on a desktop, or a rectangular area if it runs as an applet. The stage is passed as a parameter to the start method that you must override in a subclass of the Application class.

Figure 4–1   The "Hello, World" program for JavaFX

```
public class HelloWorld extends Application {
    public void start(Stage stage) {
        Label message = new Label("Hello, JavaFX!");
        message.setFont(new Font(100));
        stage.setScene(new Scene(message));
        stage.setTitle("Hello");
        stage.show();
    }
}
```

 NOTE: As you see from this example, no main method is required to launch
a JavaFX application. In previous versions of JavaFX, you were required to
include a main method of the form

```
public class MyApp extends Application {
    public static void main(String[] args) {
        launch(args);
    }
    ...
}
```

4.3 Event Handling

Graphical user interfaces are event driven. Users click on buttons, adjust sliders,
and so on. As they carry out these actions, the UI reacts and updates itself.

As in Swing, you add an event handler to a button so you can be notified when
it is clicked. Lambda expressions make this very simple:

```
Button red = new Button("Red");
red.setOnAction(event -> message.setTextFill(Color.RED));
```

When the button is clicked, the lambda is called. In this case, it sets the text color
to red.

However, with most JavaFX controls, event handling is different. Consider a
slider, as shown in Figure 4–2. When the slider is adjusted, its value changes.
However, you shouldn't listen to the low-level events that the slider emits to indicate those changes. Instead, the slider has a JavaFX *property* called value, and
the property emits events when it changes. We will discuss properties in detail
in the next section, but here is how you can listen to the property's events and
adjust the font size of the message:

```
slider.valueProperty().addListener(property
    -> message.setFont(new Font(slider.getValue())));
```

Figure 4–2   Processing slider events

Listening to properties is very common in JavaFX. For example, if you want to change a part of the user interface as a user enters text into a text field, add a listener to the text property.

 NOTE: Buttons are special. Clicking a button doesn't change one of its properties.

4.4 JavaFX Properties

A *property* is an attribute of a class that you can read or write. Commonly, the property is backed by a field, and the property getter and setter simply read and write that field. But the getter and setter can also take other actions, such as reading values from a database or sending out change notifications. In many programming languages, there is convenient syntax for invoking property getters and setters. Typically, using the property on the right-hand side of an assignments calls the getter, and using it on the left-hand side calls the setter.

```
value = obj.property;
    // In many languages (but not Java), this calls the property getter
obj.property = value; // And this calls the property setter
```

Sadly, Java does not have such syntax. But it has supported properties by convention since Java 1.1. The JavaBeans specification states that a property should be inferred from a getter/setter pair. For example, a class with methods String getText() and void setText(String newValue) is deemed to have a text property. The Introspector and BeanInfo classes in the java.beans package let you enumerate all properties of a class.

The JavaBeans specification also defines *bound properties*, where objects emit property change events when the setters are invoked. JavaFX does not make use of this part of the specification. Instead, a JavaFX property has a third method, besides the getter and setter, that returns an object implementing the Property interface. For example, a JavaFX text property has a method Property<String> textProperty(). You can attach a listener to the property object. That's different from old-fashioned JavaBeans. In JavaFX, the property object, not the bean, sends out notifications. There is a good reason for this change. Implementing bound JavaBeans properties required boilerplate code to add, remove, and fire listeners; in JavaFX it's much simpler because there are library classes that do all that work.

Let's see how we can implement a property text in a class Greeting. Here is the simplest way to do that:

```java
public class Greeting {
    private StringProperty text = new SimpleStringProperty("");
    public final StringProperty textProperty() { return text; }
    public final void setText(String newValue) { text.set(newValue); }
    public final String getText() { return text.get(); }
}
```

The StringProperty class wraps a string. It has methods for getting and setting the wrapped value and for managing listeners. As you can see, implementing a JavaFX property requires some boilerplate code, and there is unfortunately no way in Java to generate the code automatically. But at least you won't have to worry about managing listeners.

It is not a requirement to declare property getters and setters as final, but the JavaFX designers recommend it.

 NOTE: With this pattern, a property object is needed for each property, whether anyone listens to it or not. Exercise 2 explores a useful optimization for the pattern, creating the property objects lazily.

In the preceding example, we defined a StringProperty. For a primitive type property, use one of IntegerProperty, LongProperty, DoubleProperty, FloatProperty, or BooleanProperty. There are also ListProperty, MapProperty, and SetProperty classes. For everything else, use an ObjectProperty<T>. All these are abstract classes with concrete subclasses SimpleIntegerProperty, SimpleObjectProperty<T>, and so on.

 NOTE: If all you care about is managing listeners, your property methods can return objects of type ObjectProperty<T>, or even the Property<T> interface. The more specialized classes are useful to make computations with the properties, as explained in Section 4.5, "Bindings," on page 75.

NOTE: The property classes have methods getValue and setValue in addition to the get and set methods. In the StringProperty class, get is identical to getValue, and set to setValue. But for primitive types, they are different. For example, in an IntegerProperty, getValue returns an Integer, and get returns an int. Generally, use get and set unless you write generic code that needs to work with properties of any type.

There are two kinds of listeners that can be attached to a property. A ChangeListener is notified when the property value has changed, and an InvalidationListener is called when the property value *may* have changed. The distinction matters if a property is evaluated *lazily*. As you will see in the next section, some properties are computed from others, and the computation is only done when necessary. The ChangeListener callback tells you the old and new value, which means its caller has to compute the new value. The code that notifies an InvalidationListener doesn't compute the new value, but that means you might get a callback when the value hasn't actually changed.

In most situations, that difference is immaterial. It doesn't matter much whether you get the new value as a callback parameter or from the property. And usually, it is not worth worrying about computed properties that happen to stay unchanged even though one of their inputs changed. In the preceding section, I used an InvalidationListener because it made the code simpler.

 CAUTION: It is a bit tricky to use the ChangeListener interface for numeric properties. One would like to call

```
slider.valueProperty().addListener((property, oldValue, newValue)
    -> message.setFont(new Font(newValue)));
```

But that does not work. DoubleProperty implements Property<Number> and not Property<Double>. Therefore, the type for oldValue and newValue is Number and not Double, so you have to manually unbox:

```
slider.valueProperty().addListener((property, oldValue, newValue)
    -> message.setFont(new Font(newValue.doubleValue())));
```

4.5 Bindings

The raison d'être for JavaFX properties is the notion of *binding*: automatically updating one property when another one changes. Consider, for example, the application in Figure 4–3. When the user edits the top address, the bottom one is updated as well.

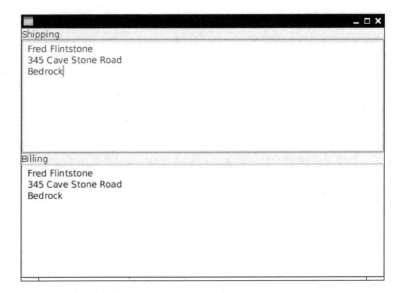

Figure 4–3   The bound text property updates automatically.

This is achieved by binding one property to the other:

```
billing.textProperty().bind(shipping.textProperty());
```

Under the hood, a change listener is added to the text property of shipping that sets the text property of billing.

You can also call

```
billing.textProperty().bindBidirectional(shipping.textProperty());
```

If either of the properties changes, the other is updated.

To undo a binding, call unbind or unbindBidirectional.

The binding mechanism solves a common problem in user interface programming. For example, consider a date field and a calendar picker. When the user picks a date from the calendar, the date field should be automatically updated, as should be the date property of the model.

Of course, in many situations, one property depends on another, but the relationship is more complex. Consider Figure 4–4. We always want the circle centered in the scene. That is, its centerX property should be one half of the width property of the scene.

To achieve this, we need to produce a computed property. The Bindings class has static methods for this purpose. For example, Bindings.divide(scene.widthProperty(), 2) is a property whose value is one half of the scene width. When the scene width

Figure 4–4   The center of this circle is bound to half the width and height of the scene.

changes, so does that property. All that remains is to bind that computed property to the circle's centerX property:

```
circle.centerXProperty().bind(Bindings.divide(scene.widthProperty(), 2));
```

> NOTE: Alternatively, you can call scene.widthProperty().divide(2). With more complex expressions, the static Bindings methods seems a bit easier to read, particularly if you use
>
> ```
> import static javafx.beans.binding.Bindings.*;
> ```
>
> and write divide(scene.widthProperty(), 2).

Here is a more realistic example. We want to disable the Smaller and Larger buttons when the gauge is too small or large (Figure 4–5).

```
smaller.disableProperty().bind(Bindings.lessThanOrEqual(gauge.widthProperty(), 0));
larger.disableProperty().bind(Bindings.greaterThanOrEqual(gauge.widthProperty(), 100));
```

When the width is ≤ 0, the Smaller button is disabled. When the width is ≥ 100, the Larger button is disabled.

Table 4–1 lists all operators that the Bindings class provides. One or both of the arguments implement the Observable interface or one of its subinterfaces. The Observable interface provides methods for adding and removing an InvalidationListener. The ObservableValue interface adds ChangeListener management and a getValue method. Its subinterfaces provide methods to get the value in the appropriate type. For example, the get method of ObservableStringValue returns a String and the get method of ObservableIntegerValue returns an int. The return types

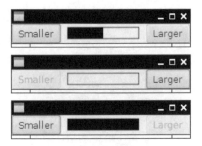

Figure 4–5   When the gauge reaches either end, a button is disabled.

of the methods of the Bindings are subinterfaces of the Binding interface, itself a subinterface of the Observable interface. A Binding knows about all properties on which it depends.

In practice, you don't need to worry about all of these interfaces. You combine properties and you get something that you can bind to another property.

Table 4–1   Operators Supplied by the Bindings Class

Method Name	Arguments
add, subtract, multiply, divide, max, min	Two of ObservableNumberValue, int, long, float, double
negate	An ObservableNumberValue
greaterThan, greaterThanOrEqual, lessThan, lessThanOrEqual	Two of ObservableNumberValue, int, long, float, double or two of ObservableStringValue, String
equal, notEqual	Two of ObservableObjectValue, ObservableNumberValue, int, long, float, double, Object
equalIgnoreCase, notEqualIgnoreCase	Two of ObservableStringValue, String
isEmpty, isNotEmpty	An Observable(List | Map | Set | StringValue)
isNull, isNotNull	An ObservableObjectValue
length	An ObservableStringValue
size	An Observable(List | Map | Set)
and, or	Two ObservableBooleanValue
not	An ObservableBooleanValue

Table 4–1 Operators Supplied by the `Bindings` Class *(Continued)*

Method Name	Arguments
`convert`	An `ObservableValue` that is converted to a string binding
`concat`	A sequence of objects whose `toString` values are concatenated. If any of the objects is an `ObservableValue` that changes, the concatenation changes too.
`format`	An optional locale, a `MessageFormat` string, and a sequence of objects that are formatted. If any of the objects is an `ObservableValue` that changes, the formatted string changes too.
`valueAt` `(double｜float｜integer｜long)ValueAt` `stringValueAt`	An `ObservableList` and an index, or an `ObservableMap` and a key
`create(Boolean｜Double｜Float｜Integer｜Long｜Object｜String)Binding`	A `Callable` and a list of dependencies
`select` `select(Boolean｜Double｜Float｜Integer｜Long｜String)`	An `Object` or `ObservableValue` and a sequence of public property names, yielding the property $obj.p_1.p_2. \ldots .p_n$
`when`	Yields a builder for a conditional operator. The binding `when(b).then(v₁).otherwise(v₂)` yields v_1 or v_2, depending on whether the `ObservableBooleanValue` b is true or not. Here, v_1 or v_2 can be regular or observable values. The conditional value is recomputed whenever an observable value changes.

Building up a computed property with the methods of the `Bindings` class can get quite baroque. There is another approach for producing computed bindings that you may find easier. Simply put the expression that you want to have computed into a lambda, and supply a list of dependent properties. When any of the properties changes, the lambda is recomputed. For example,

```
larger.disableProperty().bind(
    createBooleanBinding(
        () -> gauge.getWidth() >= 100, // This expression is computed ...
        gauge.widthProperty())); // ... when this property changes
```

Exercise 5 suggests a slightly more elegant way of lazily evaluating bindings with lambda expressions.

NOTE: In the JavaFX Script language, the compiler analyzed binding expressions and automatically figured out the dependent properties. You just declared `disable bind gauge.width >= 100`, and the compiler attached a listener to the `gauge.width` property. Of course, in Java, the programmer needs to supply this information.

4.6 Layout

When a graphical user interface contains multiple controls, they need to be arranged on the screen in a functional and attractive way. One way to obtain a layout is with a design tool. The tool's user, often a graphics designer, drags images of the controls onto a design view and arranges, resizes, and configures them. However, this approach can be problematic when the sizes of the elements change, for example, because labels have different lengths in international versions of a program.

Alternatively, the layout can be achieved programmatically, by writing code in a setup method that adds the user interface controls to specific positions. That is what was done in Swing, using layout manager objects.

Another approach is to specify the layout in a declarative language. For example, web pages are laid out with HTML and CSS. Similarly, Android has an XML language for specifying layouts.

JavaFX supports all three approaches. The JavaFX SceneBuilder is a visual GUI builder. You can download it from www.oracle.com/technetwork/java/javafx/overview. Figure 4–6 shows a screenshot.

We won't discuss the SceneBuilder program further. When you understand the concepts of this section, you will find it straightforward to use.

Programmatic layout is very similar to Swing. However, instead of layout managers that are added to arbitrary panels, one uses *panes*—containers with a layout policy. For example, a BorderPane has five areas: Top, Bottom, Left, Right, and Center. Here we place a button into each:

```
BorderPane pane = new BorderPane();
pane.setTop(new Button("Top"));
pane.setLeft(new Button("Left"));
pane.setCenter(new Button("Center"));
pane.setRight(new Button("Right"));
pane.setBottom(new Button("Bottom"));
stage.setScene(new Scene(pane));
```

Figure 4–7 shows the result.

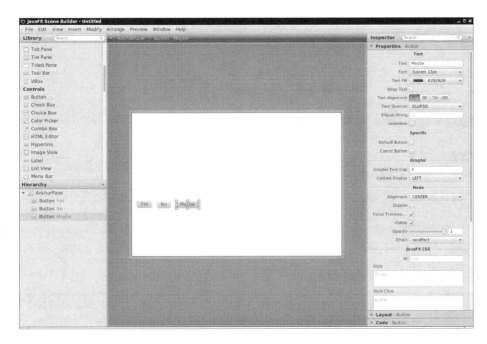

Figure 4–6   The JavaFX SceneBuilder

Figure 4–7   The BorderPane layout

 NOTE: With the Swing BorderLayout, buttons were expanded to fill each region of the layout. In JavaFX, a button does not expand past its natural size.

Now suppose you want more than one button in the South area. Use an HBox (see Figure 4–8):

```
HBox box = new HBox(10); // ten pixels between controls
box.getChildren().addAll(yesButton, noButton, maybeButton);
```

Figure 4–8   Laying out buttons with an HBox

Of course, there is a VBox for laying out controls vertically. The layout in Figure 4–8 was achieved like this:

```
VBox pane = new VBox(10);
pane.getChildren().addAll(question, buttons);
pane.setPadding(new Insets(10));
```

Note the padding property. Without it, the label and the buttons would touch the window border.

 CAUTION: In JavaFX, dimensions are specified in pixels. In our example, we use ten pixels for the box spacing and padding. This is not really appropriate nowadays, when pixel densities can vay widely. One way to overcome this is to compute dimensions in rem, as you would do in CSS3. (A rem or "root em" is the height of the default font of the document root.)

```
final double rem = new Text("").getLayoutBounds().getHeight();
pane.setPadding(new Insets(0.8 * rem));
```

There is only so much you can achieve with horizontal and vertical boxes. Just as Swing had the GridBagLayout as "the mother of all layout managers," JavaFX has the GridPane. Think of a GridPane as an equivalent of an HTML table. You can set the horizontal and vertical alignment of all cells. If desired, cells can span multiple rows and columns. Consider the login dialog in Figure 4–9.

Figure 4–9   A GridPane can arrange the controls for this login dialog.

Note the following:

- The labels "User name:" and "Password:" are right aligned.
- The buttons are in an HBox that spans two columns.

When you add a child to a GridPane, specify its column and row index (in that order; think *x*- and *y*-coordinates).

```
pane.add(usernameLabel, 0, 0);
pane.add(username, 1, 0);
pane.add(passwordLabel, 0, 1);
pane.add(password, 1, 1);
```

If a child spans multiple columns or rows, specify the spans after the positions. For example, the button panel spans two columns and one row:

```
pane.add(buttons, 0, 2, 2, 1);
```

If you want a child to span all remaining rows or columns, you can use GridPane.REMAINING.

To set the horizontal alignment of a child, use the static setHalignment method, and pass the child reference and a constant LEFT, CENTER, or RIGHT from the HPos enumeration.

```
GridPane.setHalignment(usernameLabel, HPos.RIGHT);
```

Similarly, for vertical alignment, call setValignment and use TOP, CENTER, or BOTTOM from the VPos enumeration.

NOTE: These static calls look rather inelegant in Java code, but they make sense in the FXML markup language—see the next section.

CAUTION: Do *not* center the HBox with the buttons inside the grid. That box has expanded to the full horizontal size, and centering will not change its position. Instead, tell the HBox to center its contents:

```
buttons.setAlignment(Pos.CENTER);
```

You will also want to provide some spacing around the rows and columns and some padding around the table:

```
pane.setHgap(0.8 * rem);
pane.setVgap(0.8 * rem);
pane.setPadding(new Insets(0.8 * rem));
```

TIP: For debugging, it can be useful to see the cell boundaries (see Figure 4–10). Call

```
pane.setGridLinesVisible(true);
```

If you want to see the borders of an individual child (for example, to see whether it has grown to fill the entire cell), set its border. This is most easily done with CSS:

```
buttons.setStyle("-fx-border-color: red;");
```

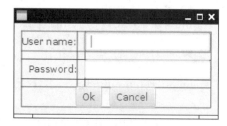

Figure 4–10   Use visible grid lines when debugging a GridPane.

These layout panes should suffice for the majority of applications. Table 4–2 shows all layouts that come with JavaFX.

Table 4–2 JavaFX Layouts

Pane Class	Description
HBox, VBox	Lines up children horizontally or vertically.
GridPane	Lays out children in a tabular grid, similar to the Swing GridBagLayout.
TilePane	Lays out children in a grid, giving them all the same size, similar to the Swing GridLayout.
BorderPane	Provides the areas Top, Bottom, Left, Right, and Center, similar to the Swing BorderLayout.
FlowPane	Flows children in rows, making new rows when there isn't sufficient space, similar to the Swing FlowLayout.
AnchorPane	Children can be positioned in absolute positions, or relative to pane's boundaries. This is the default in the SceneBuilder layout tool.
StackPane	Stacks children above each other. Can be useful for decorating components, such as stacking a button over a colored rectangle.

NOTE: In this section, we built up user interfaces by manually nesting panes and controls. JavaFX Script had a "builder" syntax for describing such nested structures (called the "scene graph"). JavaFX 2 used builder classes to imitate that syntax. Here is how to build up the login dialog:

```
GridPane pane = GridPaneBuilder.create()
    .hgap(10)
    .vgap(10)
    .padding(new Insets(10))
    .children(
        usernameLabel = LabelBuilder.create()
        .text("User name:")
        .build(),
        passwordLabel = LabelBuilder.create()
        .text("Password:")
        .build(),
        username = TextFieldBuilder.create().build(),
        password = PasswordFieldBuilder.create().build(),
        buttons = HBoxBuilder.create()
        .spacing(10)
        .alignment(Pos.CENTER)
        .children(
            okButton = ButtonBuilder.create()
            .text("Ok")
            .build(),
            cancelButton = ButtonBuilder.create()
            .text("Cancel")
            .build())
        .build())
    .build();
```

That's amazingly verbose, and it's not even the full story—one still needed to specify the grid constraints. Builders have been deprecated in JavaFX 8, not because they are so verbose, but because of an implementation issue. To save code, builders have an inheritance tree that parallels the inheritance of the corresponding nodes. For example, GridPaneBuilder extends PaneBuilder because GridPane extends Pane. But now you have a problem. What should PaneBuilder.children return? If it only returns a PaneBuilder, then the user has to be very careful to first configure the subclass properties, then the super-class properties. The JavaFX designers tried to solve this problem with generics. The methods of a PaneBuilder<B> return a B, so that a GridPaneBuilder can extend PaneBuilder<GridPaneBuilder>. Wait, that can't work—GridPaneBuilder is itself generic, so that would have to be a GridPaneBuilder<GridPaneBuilder>, or really a GridPaneBuilder<GridPaneBuilder<something>>. This circularity was overcome with some tricks, but those tricks are unsound, and they won't work in future versions of Java. Thus, builders were withdrawn.

If you like builders, you can use Scala or Groovy and their JavaFX bindings (https://code.google.com/p/scalafx, http://groovyfx.org).

4.7 FXML

The markup language that JavaFX uses to describe layouts is called FXML. I discuss it in some detail because the concepts are interesting beyond the needs of JavaFX, and the implementation is fairly general.

Here is the FXML markup for the login dialog of the preceding section:

```
<?xml version="1.0" encoding="UTF-8"?>

<?import java.lang.*?>
<?import java.util.*?>
<?import javafx.scene.control.*?>
<?import javafx.scene.layout.*?>

<GridPane hgap="10" vgap="10">
    <padding>
        <Insets top="10" right="10" bottom="10" left="10"/>
    </padding>
    <children>
        <Label text="User name:" GridPane.columnIndex="0" GridPane.rowIndex="0"
            GridPane.halignment="RIGHT" />
        <Label text="Password: " GridPane.columnIndex="0" GridPane.rowIndex="1"
            GridPane.halignment="RIGHT" />
        <TextField GridPane.columnIndex="1" GridPane.rowIndex="0"/>
        <PasswordField GridPane.columnIndex="1" GridPane.rowIndex="1" />
        <HBox GridPane.columnIndex="0" GridPane.rowIndex="2"
            GridPane.columnSpan="2" alignment="CENTER" spacing="10">
            <children>
                <Button text="Ok" />
                <Button text="Cancel" />
            </children>
        </HBox>
    </children>
</GridPane>
```

Have a closer look at the FXML file. Note the "processing instructions" <?import ...?> for importing Java packages. (In general, XML processing instructions are an "escape hatch" for application-specific processing of XML documents.)

Now look at the structure of the document. First off, the nesting of the GridPane, the labels and text fields, the HBox and its button children reflects the nesting that we built up with Java code in the preceding section.

Most of the attributes correspond to property setters. For example,

```
<GridPane hgap="10" vgap="10">
```

means "construct a GridPane and then set the hgap and vgap properties."

When an attribute starts with a class name and a static method, that method is invoked. For example,

```
<TextField GridPane.columnIndex="1" GridPane.rowIndex="0"/>
```

means that the static methods GridPane.setColumnIndex(thisTextField, 1) and GridPane. setRowIndex(thisTextField, 0) will be called.

 NOTE: Generally, an FXML element is constructed with its default constructor and then customized by calling property setters or static methods, in the spirit of the JavaBeans specification. There are a few exceptions that we will consider later.

When a property value is too complex to express as a string, one uses nested elements instead of attributes. Consider, for example,

```
<GridPane hgap="10" vgap="10">
   <padding>
      <Insets top="10" right="10" bottom="10" left="10"/>
   </padding>
   ...
```

The padding property has type Insets, and the Insets object is constructed with an <Insets ...> child element that specifies how to set its properties.

Finally, there is a special rule for list properties. For example, children is a list property, and calling

```
<HBox ...>
   <children>
      <Button text="Ok" />
      <Button text="Cancel" />
   </children>
</HBox>
```

adds the buttons to the list returned by getChildren.

You can write FXML files by hand, or you can use the SceneBuilder program that I mentioned in the preceding section. Once you have such a file, load it like this:

```
public void start(Stage stage) {
   try {
      Parent root = FXMLLoader.load(getClass().getResource("dialog.fxml"));
      stage.setScene(new Scene(root));
      stage.show();
   } catch (IOException ex) {
      ex.printStackTrace();
       System.exit(0);
   }
}
```

Of course, this is not yet useful by itself. The user interface is displayed, but the program cannot access the values that the user provides. One way of establishing a connection between the controls and the program is to use id attributes, as you would in JavaScript. Provide the id attributes in the FXML file:

```
<TextField id="username" GridPane.columnIndex="1" GridPane.rowIndex="0"/>
```

In the program, look up the control:

```
TextField username = (TextField) root.lookup("#username");
```

But there is a better way. You can use the @FXML annotation to "inject" the control objects into a *controller* class. The controller class must implement the Initializable interface. In the controller's initialize method, you wire up the binders and event handlers. Any class can be the controller, even the FX application itself.

For example, here is a controller for our login dialog:

```
public class LoginDialogController implements Initializable {
   @FXML private TextField username;
   @FXML private PasswordField password;
   @FXML private Button okButton;

   public void initialize(URL url, ResourceBundle rb) {
      okButton.disableProperty().bind(
         Bindings.createBooleanBinding(
            () -> username.getText().length() == 0
               || password.getText().length() == 0,
            username.textProperty(),
            password.textProperty()));
      okButton.setOnAction(event ->
         System.out.println("Verifying " + username.getText()
            + ":" + password.getText()));
   }
```

In the FXML file, provide the names of the controller's instance variables to the corresponding control elements in the FXML file, using the fx:id (not id) attribute:

```
<TextField fx:id="username" GridPane.columnIndex="1" GridPane.rowIndex="0"/>
<PasswordField fx:id="password" GridPane.columnIndex="1" GridPane.rowIndex="1" />
<Button fx:id="okButton" text="Ok" />
```

In the root element, you also need to declare the controller class, using the fx:controller attribute:

```
<GridPane xmlns:fx="http://javafx.com/fxml" hgap="10" vgap="10"
    fx:controller="LoginDialogController">
```

Note the namespace attribute to introduce the FXML namespace.

NOTE: If your controller doesn't have a default constructor (perhaps, because it is being initialized with a reference to a business service), you can set it programmatically:

```
FXMLLoader loader = new FXMLLoader(getClass().getResource(...));
loader.setController(new Controller(service));
Parent root = (Parent) loader.load();
```

CAUTION: If you set the controller programmatically, really use the code from the preceding note. The following code will compile, but it will invoke the static FXMLLoader.load method, ignoring the constructed loader:

```
FXMLLoader loader = new FXMLLoader();
loader.setController(...);
Parent root = (Parent) loader.load(getClass().getResource(...));
    // Error—calls static method
```

When the FXML file is loaded, the scene graph is constructed, and references to the named control objects are injected into the annotated fields of the controller object. Then its initialize method is called.

It is even possible do much of the initialization in the FXML file. You can define simple bindings, and you can set annotated controller methods as event listeners. The syntax is documented at http://docs.oracle.com/javafx/2/api/javafx/fxml/doc-files/introduction_to_fxml.html. However, let's not dwell on these features. It seems better to separate the visual design from the program behavior, so that a user interface designer can produce the design and a programmer can implement the behavior.

NOTE: It is also possible to add scripts in JavaScript or another scripting language to an FXML file. We will discuss this briefly in Chapter 7.

4.8 CSS

JavaFX lets you change the visual appearance of the user interface with CSS, which is usually more convenient than supplying FXML attributes or calling Java methods.

You can load a CSS style sheet programmatically and have it applied to a scene graph:

```
Scene scene = new Scene(pane);
scene.getStylesheets().add("scene.css");
```

In the style sheet, you can reference any controls that have an ID. For example, here is how you can control the appearance of a GridPane. In the code, set the ID:

```
GridPane pane = new GridPane();
pane.setId("pane");
```

Don't set any padding or spacing in the code. Instead, use CSS.

```
#pane {
    -fx-padding: 0.5em;
    -fx-hgap: 0.5em;
    -fx-vgap: 0.5em;
    -fx-background-image: url("metal.jpg")
}
```

Unfortunately, you can't use the familiar CSS attributes but need to know FX-specific attributes that start with -fx-. The attribute names are formed by changing the property names to lowercase and using hyphens instead of camel case. For example, the textAlignment property turns into -fx-text-alignment. You can find all supported attributes in the JavaFX CSS reference at http://docs.oracle.com/ javafx/2/api/javafx/scene/doc-files/cssref.html.

Using CSS is nicer than cluttering up the code with layout minutiae. Moreover, you can easily use resolution-independent em units. Of course CSS can be used both for good and for evil (see Figure 4–11), and I hope you will resist the temptation to apply gratuitous background textures to your login dialogs.

Instead of styling by individual IDs, you can use style classes. Add the class to the node object:

```
HBox buttons = new HBox();
buttons.getStyleClass().add("buttonrow");
```

Then style it, using the CSS class notation:

Figure 4–11   Using CSS to style a user interface

```
.buttonrow {
    -fx-spacing: 0.5em;
}
```

Every JavaFX control and shape class belongs to a CSS class whose name is the decapitalized Java class name. For example, all Label nodes have class label. Here is how you can change the font for all labels to Comic Sans:

```
.label {
    -fx-font-family: "Comic Sans MS";
}
```

But please don't.

You can also use CSS with FXML layouts. Attach the stylesheet to the root pane:

```
<GridPane id="pane" stylesheets="scene.css">
```

Supply id or styleClass attributes in the FXML code. For example,

```
<HBox styleClass="buttonrow">
```

Then you can specify most styling in CSS, and use FXML only for layout. Unfortunately, you can't completely remove all styling from the FXML. For example, there is currently no way to specify grid cell alignment in CSS.

 NOTE: You can also apply a CSS style programmatically, such as

```
buttons.setStyle("-fx-border-color: red;");
```

That can be handy for debugging, but in general, it seems better to use an external stylesheet.

4.9 Animations and Special Effects

When JavaFX was born, special effects were all the rage, and JavaFX makes it easy to produce shadows, blurs, and movement. You will find dozens of pretty

Figure 4–12   Buttons that grow, fade, and turn

demos on the Web with swirling bubbles moving aimlessly, text jumping nervously, and so on. I thought you'd enjoy some useful tips on how to bring these animations to the world of business applications. Figure 4–12 shows an application where the Yes button increases in size while the No button fades into the background and the Maybe button rotates.

JavaFX defines a number of *transitions* that, over a period of time, vary a property of a node. Here is how you grow a node by 50% in both x and y directions over three seconds:

```
ScaleTransition st = new ScaleTransition(Duration.millis(3000));
st.setByX(1.5);
st.setByY(1.5);
st.setNode(yesButton);
st.play();
```

The node can be any node in a scene graph, such as a circle in an animation of soap bubbles or the ever more enticing Yes button in our example.

As set up, the transition will end when its goal is met. You can cycle it indefinitely like this:

```
st.setCycleCount(Animation.INDEFINITE);
st.setAutoReverse(true);
```

Now the node will get bigger, then smaller, then bigger again, and so on.

The FadeTransition changes the opacity of a node. Here is how the No button fades into the background:

```
FadeTransition ft = new FadeTransition(Duration.millis(3000));
ft.setFromValue(1.0);
ft.setToValue(0);
ft.setNode(noButton);
ft.play();
```

All JavaFX nodes can be rotated around their center. The RotateTransition changes the node's rotate property. The following code animates the rotation of the Maybe button:

```
RotateTransition rt = new RotateTransition(Duration.millis(3000));
rt.setByAngle(180);
rt.setCycleCount(Animation.INDEFINITE);
rt.setAutoReverse(true);
rt.setNode(maybeButton);
rt.play();
```

You can compose transitions with the ParallelTransition and SequentialTransition combinators, performing them in parallel or one after the other. If you need to animate multiple nodes, you can place them into a Group node and animate that. When you need to create this kind of behavior, the JavaFX classes are a joy to work with.

Special effects are also very easy to do. If you need a drop shadow for a spiffy caption, make a DropShadow effect and set it as the effect property of a node. Figure 4–13 shows the result with a Text node. Here is the code:

```
DropShadow dropShadow = new DropShadow();
dropShadow.setRadius(5.0);
dropShadow.setOffsetX(3.0);
dropShadow.setOffsetY(3.0);
dropShadow.setColor(Color.GRAY);

Text text = new Text();
text.setFill(Color.RED);
text.setText("Drop shadow");
text.setFont(Font.font("sans", FontWeight.BOLD, 40));
text.setEffect(dropShadow);
```

Figure 4–13   JavaFX effects

To set a glow or a blur effect is just as simple:

```
text2.setEffect(new Glow(0.8));
text3.setEffect(new GaussianBlur());
```

Admittedly, the glow effect looks a bit cheesy and the blur effect doesn't seem to have many applications in the world of business, but it is impressive how easy it is to produce these effects.

4.10 Fancy Controls

Of course, JavaFX has combo boxes, tab panes, trees, and tables, just like Swing does, as well as a few user interface controls that Swing never got, such as a date picker and an accordion. It would take an entire book to describe these in detail. In this section, I want to dispel any remaining Swing nostalgia by showing you three fancy controls that are far beyond what Swing had to offer.

Figure 4–14 shows one of many charts that you can make with JavaFX, out of the box, without having to install any third-party libraries.

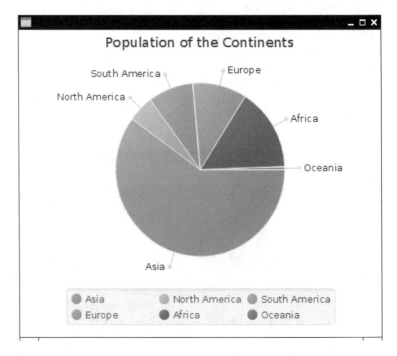

Figure 4–14 A JavaFX pie chart

And it's easy as pie:

```
ObservableList<PieChart.Data> pieChartData =
    FXCollections.observableArrayList(
        new PieChart.Data("Asia", 4298723000.0),
        new PieChart.Data("North America", 355361000.0),
        new PieChart.Data("South America", 616644000.0),
        new PieChart.Data("Europe", 742452000.0),
        new PieChart.Data("Africa", 1110635000.0),
        new PieChart.Data("Oceania", 38304000.0));
final PieChart chart = new PieChart(pieChartData);
chart.setTitle("Population of the Continents");
```

Altogether, there are half a dozen chart types that you can use and customize. See http://docs.oracle.com/javafx/2/charts/chart-overview.htm for more information.

In Swing, you could show HTML in a JEditorPane, but the rendering was poor for most real-world HTML. That's understandable—implementing a browser is hard work. In fact, it is so hard that most browsers are built on top of the open source WebKit engine. JavaFX does the same. A WebView displays an embedded native WebKit window (see Figure 4–15).

Here is the code to show a web page:

```
String location = "http://horstmann.com";
WebView browser = new WebView();
WebEngine engine = browser.getEngine();
engine.load(location);
```

The browser is live—you can click on links in the usual way. JavaScript works as well. However, if you want to display status line or popup messages from JavaScript, you need to install notification handlers and implement your own status line and popups.

 NOTE: WebView does not support any plugins, so you cannot use it to show Flash animations or PDF documents. It also doesn't show applets.

Prior to JavaFX, media playback was pitiful in Java. A Java Media Framework was available as an optional download, but it did not get much love from the developers. Of course, implementing audio and video playback is even harder than writing a browser. Therefore, JavaFX leverages an existing toolkit, the open source GStreamer framework.

To play a video, construct a Media object from an URL string, construct a MediaPlayer to play it, and a MediaView to show the player:

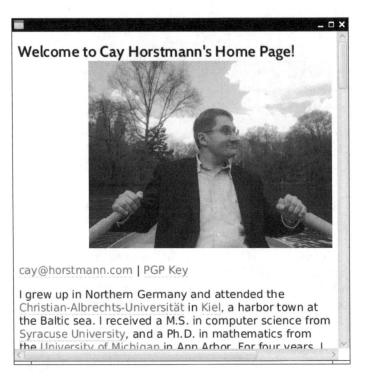

Figure 4–15   Browsing the Web

```
Path path = Paths.get("moonlanding.mp4");
String location = path.toUri().toString();
Media media = new Media(location);
MediaPlayer player = new MediaPlayer(media);
player.setAutoPlay(true);
MediaView view = new MediaView(player);
view.setOnError(e -> System.out.println(e));
```

As you can see in Figure 4–16, the video is played—but, unfortunately, there are no video controls. You can add your own (see http://docs.oracle.com/javafx/2/media/playercontrol.htm, but it would have been nice to supply a default set of controls.

 NOTE: Ever so often, GStreamer can't handle a particular video file. The error handler in the code sample displays GStreamer messages so that you can diagnose playback problems.

Figure 4–16 Playing a video

That brings us to the end of this quick tour through JavaFX. JavaFX is the future of desktop Java. It has a few rough edges, mostly due to a hurried transformation from the original scripting language. But it is certainly no harder to use than Swing, and it has many more useful and attractive controls than Swing ever had.

Exercises

1. Write a program with a text field and a label. As with the Hello, JavaFX program, the label should have the string Hello, FX in a 100 point font. Initialize the text field with the same string. Update the label as the user edits the text field.

2. Consider a class with many JavaFX properties, such as a chart or table. Chances are that in a particular application, most properties never have listeners attached to them. It is therefore wasteful to have a property object per property. Show how the property can be set up on demand, first using a regular field for storing the property value, and then using a property object only when the *xxx*Property() method is called for the first time.

3. Consider a class with many JavaFX properties, most of which are never changed from a default. Show how the property can be set up on demand, when it is set to a nondefault value or when the *xxx*Property() method is called for the first time.

4. Enhance the program in Section 4.5, "Bindings," on page 75 so that the circle stays centered and always touches at least two of the sides of the scene.

5. Write methods

```
public static <T, R> ObservableValue<R> observe(
    Function<T, R> f, ObservableValue<T> t)
public static <T, U, R> ObservableValue<R> observe(
    BiFunction<T, U, R> f, ObservableValue<T> t, ObservableValue<U> u)
```

that return observable values whose getValue method returns the value of the lambda expression, and whose invalidation and change listeners are fired when any of the inputs become invalid or change. For example,

```
larger.disableProperty().bind(observe(
    t -> t >= 100, gauge.widthProperty()));
```

6. Center the top and bottom buttons in Figure 4–7.

7. Find out how to set the border of a control without using CSS.

8. Since there is no JavaFX-specific knowledge in parsing FXML files, come up with an example where you load an object that has nothing to do with JavaFX, with some nested objects, and set the properties in FXML syntax. Extra credit if you use injection.

9. Animate a circle, representing a planet, so it travels along an elliptical orbit. Use a PathTransition.

10. Using the web viewer, implement a browser with a URL bar and a back button. Hint: WebEngine.getHistory().

The New Date and Time API

Chapter 5

Time flies like an arrow, and we can easily set a starting point and count forward and backwards in seconds. So why is it so hard to deal with time? The problem is humans. All would be easy if we could just tell each other: "Meet me at 1371409200, and don't be late!" But we want time to relate to daylight and the seasons. That's where things get complicated. Java 1.0 had a Date class that was, in hindsight, unbelievably naïve, and had most of its methods deprecated in Java 1.1 when a Calendar class was introduced. Its API wasn't stellar, its instances were mutable, and it didn't deal with issues such as leap seconds. The third time is a charm, and the java.time API that is introduced in Java 8 has remedied the flaws of the past and should serve us for quite some time. In this chapter, you will learn what makes time computations so vexing, and how the new Date and Time API solves these issues.

The key points of this chapter are:

- All java.time objects are immutable.
- An Instant is a point on the time line (similar to a Date).
- In Java time, each day has exactly 86,400 seconds (i.e., no leap seconds).
- A Duration is the difference between two instants.
- LocalDateTime has no time zone information.
- TemporalAdjuster methods handle common calendar computations, such as finding the first Tuesday of a month.

- ZonedDateTime is a point in time in a given time zone (similar to GregorianCalendar).

- Use a Period, not a Duration, when advancing zoned time, in order to account for daylight savings time changes.

- Use DateTimeFormatter to format and parse dates and times.

5.1 The Time Line

Historically, the fundamental time unit, the second, was derived from Earth's rotation around its axis. There are 24 hours or 24 × 60 × 60 = 86400 seconds in a full revolution, so it seems just a question of astronomical measurements to precisely define a second. Unfortunately, Earth wobbles slightly, and a more precise definition was needed. In 1967, a new precise definition of a second, matching the historical definition, was derived from an intrinsic property of atoms of caesium-133. Since then, a network of atomic clocks keeps the official time.

Ever so often, the official time keepers synchronize the absolute time with the rotation of Earth. At first, the official seconds were slightly adjusted, but starting in 1972, "leap seconds" were occasionally inserted. (In theory, a second might need to be removed once in a while, but that has not yet happened.) There is talk of changing the system again. Clearly, leap seconds are a pain, and many computer systems instead use "smoothing" where time is artificially slowed down or sped up just before the leap second, keeping 86,400 seconds per day. This works because the local time on a computer isn't all that precise, and computers are used to synchronizing themselves with an external time service.

The Java Date and Time API specification requires that Java uses a time scale that

- Has 86,400 seconds per day

- Exactly matches the official time at noon each day

- Closely matches it elsewhere, in a precisely defined way

That gives Java the flexibility to adjust to future changes in the official time.

In Java, an Instant represents a point on the time line. An origin, called the *epoch*, is arbitrarily set at midnight of January 1, 1970 at the prime meridian that passes through the Greenwich Royal Observatory in London. This is the same convention used in the Unix/POSIX time. Starting from that origin, time is measured in 86,400 seconds per day, forwards and backwards, in nanosecond precision. The Instant values go back as far as a billion years (Instant.MIN). That's not quite enough to express the age of the universe (around 13.5 billion years), but it should be enough for all practical purposes. After all, a billion years ago, the earth was covered in ice and populated by microscopic ancestors of today's plants and animals. The largest value, Instant.MAX, is December 31 of the year 1,000,000,000. The static method call Instant.now() gives the current instant. You can compare two instants with the equals and compareTo methods in the usual way, so you can use instants as timestamps.

To find out the difference between two instants, use the static method Duration.between. For example, here is how you can measure the running time of an algorithm:

```
Instant start = Instant.now();
runAlgorithm();
Instant end = Instant.now();
Duration timeElapsed = Duration.between(start, end);
long millis = timeElapsed.toMillis();
```

A Duration is the amount of time between two instants. You can get the length of a Duration in conventional units by calling toNanos, toMillis, toSeconds, toMinutes, toHours, or toDays.

Durations require more than a long value for their internal storage. The number of seconds is stored in a long, and the number of nanoseconds in an additional int. If you want to make computations in nanosecond accuracy, and you actually need the entire range of a Duration, then you can use one of the methods in Table 5–1. Otherwise, you can just call toNanos and do your calculations with long values.

 NOTE: It takes almost 300 years of nanoseconds to overflow a long.

Table 5–1 Arithmetic Operations for Time Instants and Durations

Method	Description
plus, minus	Adds a duration to, or subtracts a duration from, this Instant or Duration.
plusNanos, plusMillis, plusSeconds, plusMinutes, plusHours, plusDays	Adds a number of the given time units to this Instant or Duration.
minusNanos, minusMillis, minusSeconds, minusMinutes, minusHours, minusDays	Subtracts a number of the given time units from this Instant or Duration.
multipliedBy, dividedBy, negated	Returns a duration that is obtained by multiplying or dividing this Duration by a given long, or by –1. Note that you can scale only durations, not instants.
isZero, isNegative	Checks whether this Duration is zero or negative.

For example, if you want to check whether an algorithm is at least ten times faster than another, you can compute

```
Duration timeElapsed2 = Duration.between(start2, end2);
boolean overTenTimesFaster =
    timeElapsed.multipliedBy(10).minus(timeElapsed2).isNegative();
    // Or timeElapsed.toNanos() * 10 < timeElapsed2.toNanos()
```

NOTE: The Instant and Duration classes are immutable, and all methods, such as multipliedBy or minus, return a new instance.

5.2 Local Dates

Now let us turn from absolute time to human time. There are two kinds of human time in the new Java API, *local date/time* and *zoned time*. Local date/time has a date and/or time of day, but no associated time zone information. A local date is, for example, June 14, 1903 (the day on which Alonzo Church, inventor of the lambda calculus, was born). Since that date has neither a time of day nor time zone information, it does not correspond to a precise instant of time. In contrast, July 16, 1969, 09:32:00 EDT (the launch of Apollo 11) is a zoned date/time, representing a precise instant on the time line.

There are many calculations where time zones are not required, and in some cases they can even be a hindrance. Suppose you schedule a meeting every week at 10:00. If you add 7 days (that is, $7 \times 24 \times 60 \times 60$ seconds) to the last zoned time, and you happen to cross the daylight savings time boundary, the meeting will be an hour too early or too late!

For that reason, the API designers recommend that you do not use zoned time unless you really want to represent absolute time instances. Birthdays, holidays, schedule times, and so on are usually best represented as local dates or times.

A LocalDate is a date, with a year, month, and day of the month. To construct one, you can use the now or of static methods:

```
LocalDate today = LocalDate.now(); // Today's date
LocalDate alonzosBirthday = LocalDate.of(1903, 6, 14);
alonzosBirthday = LocalDate.of(1903, Month.JUNE, 14);
    // Uses the Month enumeration
```

Unlike the irregular conventions in Unix and java.util.Date, where months are zero-based and years are counted from 1900, you supply the usual numbers for the month of year. Alternatively, you can use the Month enumeration.

Table 5–2 shows the most useful methods for working with LocalDate objects.

Table 5–2 LocalDate Methods

Method	Description
now, of	These static methods construct a LocalDate, either from the current time or from a given year, month, and day.
plusDays, plusWeeks, plusMonths, plusYears	Adds a number of days, weeks, months, or years to this LocalDate.
minusDays, minusWeeks, minusMonths, minusYears	Subtracts a number of days, weeks, months, or years from this LocalDate.
plus, minus	Adds or subtracts a Duration or Period.
withDayOfMonth, withDayOfYear, withMonth, withYear	Returns a new LocalDate with the day of month, day of year, month, or year changed to the given value.
getDayOfMonth	Gets the day of the month (between 1 and 31).
getDayOfYear	Gets the day of the year (between 1 and 366).
getDayOfWeek	Gets the day of the week, returning a value of the DayOfWeek enumeration.
getMonth, getMonthValue	Gets the month as a value of the Month enumeration, or as a number between 1 and 12.
getYear	Gets the year, between –999,999,999 and 999,999,999.
until	Gets the Period, or the number of the given ChronoUnits, between two dates.
isBefore, isAfter	Compares this LocalDate with another.
isLeapYear	Returns true if the year is a leap year—that is, if it is divisible by 4 but not by 100, or divisible by 400. The algorithm is applied for all past years, even though that is historically inaccurate. (Leap years were invented in the year –46, and the rules involving divisibility by 100 and 400 were introduced in the Gregorian calendar reform of 1582. The reform took over 300 years to become universal.)

For example, *Programmer's Day* is the 256th day of the year. Here is how you can easily compute it:

```
LocalDate programmersDay = LocalDate.of(2014, 1, 1).plusDays(255);
   // September 13, but in a leap year it would be September 12
```

Recall that the difference between two time instants is a Duration. The equivalent for local dates is a Period, which expresses a number of elapsed years, months, or days. You can call birthday.plus(Period.ofYears(1)), to get the birthday next year. Of course, you can also just call birthday.plusYears(1). But birthday.plus(Duration.ofDays(365)) won't produce the correct result in a leap year.

The until method yields the difference between two local dates. For example,

```
independenceDay.until(christmas)
```

yields a period of 5 months and 21 days. That is actually not terribly useful because the number of days per month varies. To find the number of days, use

```
independenceDay.until(christmas, ChronoUnit.DAYS) // 174 days
```

 CAUTION: Some methods in Table 5–2 could potentially create nonexistent dates. For example, adding one month to January 31 should not yield February 31. Instead of throwing an exception, these methods return the last valid day of the month. For example,

```
LocalDate.of(2016, 1, 31).plusMonths(1)
```

and

```
LocalDate.of(2016, 3, 31).minusMonths(1)
```

yield February 29, 2016.

The getDayOfWeek yields the weekday, as a value of the DayOfWeek enumeration. DayOfWeek.MONDAY has the numerical value 1, and DayOfWeek.SUNDAY has the value 7. For example,

```
LocalDate.of(1900, 1, 1).getDayOfWeek().getValue()
```

yields 1. The DayOfWeek enumeration has convenience methods plus and minus to compute weekdays modulo 7. For example, DayOfWeek.SATURDAY.plus(3) yields DayOfWeek.TUESDAY.

 NOTE: The weekend days actually come at the end of the week. This is different from java.util.Calendar, where Sunday has value 1 and Saturday value 7.

In addition to LocalDate, there are also classes MonthDay, YearMonth, and Year to describe partial dates. For example, December 25 (with the year unspecified) can be represented as a MonthDay.

5.3 Date Adjusters

For scheduling applications, you often need to compute dates such as "the first Tuesday of every month." The TemporalAdjusters class provides a number of static methods for common adjustments. You pass the result of an adjustment method to the with method. For example, the first Tuesday of a month can be computed like this:

```
LocalDate firstTuesday = LocalDate.of(year, month, 1).with(
    TemporalAdjusters.nextOrSame(DayOfWeek.TUESDAY));
```

As always, the with method returns a new LocalDate object without modifying the original. Table 5–3 shows the available adjusters.

You can also roll your own adjuster by implementing the TemporalAdjuster interface. Here is an adjuster for computing the next weekday.

```
TemporalAdjuster NEXT_WORKDAY = w -> {
    LocalDate result = (LocalDate) w;
    do {
        result = result.plusDays(1);
    } while (result.getDayOfWeek().getValue() >= 6);
    return result;
};

LocalDate backToWork = today.with(NEXT_WORKDAY);
```

Note that the parameter of the lambda expression has type Temporal, and it must be cast to LocalDate. You can avoid this cast with the ofDateAdjuster method that expects a lambda of type UnaryOperator<LocalDate>.

Table 5–3 Date Adjusters in the TemporalAdjusters Class

Method	Description
next(weekday), previous(weekday)	Next or previous date that falls on the given weekday
nextOrSame(weekday), previousOrSame(weekday)	Next or previous date that falls on the given weekday, starting from the given date
dayOfWeekInMonth(n, weekday)	The nth weekday in the month
lastInMonth(weekday)	The last weekday in the month
firstDayOfMonth(), firstDayOfNextMonth(), firstDayOfNextYear(), lastDayOfMonth(), lastDayOfPreviousMonth(), lastDayOfYear()	The date described in the method name

```
TemporalAdjuster NEXT_WORKDAY = TemporalAdjusters.ofDateAdjuster(w -> {
   LocalDate result = w; // No cast
   do {
      result = result.plusDays(1);
   } while (result.getDayOfWeek().getValue() >= 6);
   return result;
});
```

5.4 Local Time

A LocalTime represents a time of day, such as 15:30:00. You can create an instance with the now or of methods:

```
LocalTime rightNow = LocalTime.now();
LocalTime bedtime = LocalTime.of(22, 30); // or LocalTime.of(22, 30, 0)
```

Table 5–4 shows common operations with local times. The plus and minus operations wrap around a 24-hour day. For example,

```
LocalTime wakeup = bedtime.plusHours(8); // wakeup is 6:30:00
```

Table 5–4 LocalTime Methods

Method	Description
now, of	These static methods construct a LocalTime, either from the current time, or from the given hours, minutes, and optionally, seconds and nanoseconds.
plusHours, plusMinutes, plusSeconds, plusNanos	Adds a number of hours, minutes, seconds, or nanoseconds to this LocalTime.
minusHours, minusMinutes, minusSeconds, minusNanos	Subtracts a number of hours, minutes, seconds, or nanoseconds from this LocalTime.
plus, minus	Adds or subtracts a Duration.
withHour, withMinute, withSecond, withNano	Returns a new LocalTime with the hour, minute, second, or nanosecond changed to the given value.
getHour, getMinute, getSecond, getNano	Gets the hour, minute, second, or nanosecond of this LocalTime.
toSecondOfDay, toNanoOfDay	Returns the number of seconds or nanoseconds between midnight and this LocalTime.
isBefore, isAfter	Compares this LocalTime with another.

NOTE: LocalTime doesn't concern itself with AM/PM. That silliness is left to a formatter—see Section 5.6, "Formatting and Parsing," on page 112.

There is a LocalDateTime class, representing a date and time. That class is suitable for storing points in time in a fixed time zone, for example, for a schedule of classes or events. However, if you need to make calculations that span the daylight savings time, or if you need to deal with users in different time zones, you should use the ZonedDateTime class that we discuss next.

5.5 Zoned Time

Time zones, perhaps because they are an entirely human creation, are even messier than the complications caused by the earth's irregular rotation. In a rational world, we'd all follow the clock in Greenwich, and some of us would eat our lunch at 02:00, others at 22:00. Our stomachs would figure it out. This is actually done in China, which spans four conventional time zones. Elsewhere, we have time zones with irregular and shifting boundaries, and, to make matters worse, the daylight savings time.

As capricious as the time zones may appear to the enlightened, they are a fact of life. When you implement a calendar application, it needs to work for people who fly from one country to another. When you have a conference call at 10:00 in New York, but happen to be in Berlin, you expect to be alerted at the correct local time.

The Internet Assigned Numbers Authority (IANA) keeps a database of all known time zones around the world (https://www.iana.org/time-zones), which is updated several times per year. The bulk of the updates deals with the changing rules for daylight savings time. Java uses the IANA database.

Each time zone has an ID, such as America/New_York or Europe/Berlin. To find out all available time zones, call ZoneId.getAvailableIds. At the time of this writing, there were almost 600 IDs.

Given a time zone ID, the static method ZoneId.of(id) yields a ZoneId object. You can use that object to turn a LocalDateTime object into a ZonedDateTime object by calling local.atZone(zoneId), or you can construct a ZonedDateTime by calling the static method ZonedDateTime.of(year, month, day, hour, minute, second, nano, zoneId). For example,

```
ZonedDateTime apollo11launch = ZonedDateTime.of(1969, 7, 16, 9, 32, 0, 0,
    ZoneId.of("America/New_York"));
    // 1969-07-16T09:32-04:00[America/New_York]
```

This is a specific instant in time. Call apollo11launch.toInstant to get the Instant. Conversely, if you have an instant in time, call instant.atZone(ZoneId.of("UTC")) to get the ZonedDateTime at the Greenwich Royal Observatory, or use another ZoneId to get it elsewhere on the planet.

 NOTE: UTC stands for "coordinated universal time," and the acronym is a compromise between the aforementioned English and the French "temps universel coordiné," having the distinction of being incorrect in either language. UTC is the time at the Greenwich Royal Observatory, without daylight savings time.

Many of the methods of ZonedDateTime are the same as those of LocalDateTime (see Table 5–5). Most are straightforward, but daylight savings time introduces some complications.

When daylight savings time starts, clocks advance by an hour. What happens when you construct a time that falls into the skipped hour? For example, in 2013, Central Europe switched to daylight savings time on March 31 at 2:00. If you try to construct nonexistent time March 31 2:30, you actually get 3:30.

```
ZonedDateTime skipped = ZonedDateTime.of(
    LocalDate.of(2013, 3, 31),
    LocalTime.of(2, 30),
    ZoneId.of("Europe/Berlin"));
    // Constructs March 31 3:30
```

Conversely, when daylight time ends, clocks are set back by an hour, and there are two instants with the same local time! When you construct a time within that span, you get the earlier of the two.

```
ZonedDateTime ambiguous = ZonedDateTime.of(
    LocalDate.of(2013, 10, 27), // End of daylight savings time
    LocalTime.of(2, 30),
    ZoneId.of("Europe/Berlin"));
    // 2013-10-27T02:30+02:00[Europe/Berlin]
ZonedDateTime anHourLater = ambiguous.plusHours(1);
    // 2013-10-27T02:30+01:00[Europe/Berlin]
```

An hour later, the time has the same hours and minutes, but the zone offset has changed.

You also need to pay attention when adjusting a date across daylight savings time boundaries. For example, if you set a meeting for next week, don't add a duration of seven days:

```
ZonedDateTime nextMeeting = meeting.plus(Duration.ofDays(7));
    // Caution! Won't work with daylight savings time
```

Instead, use the Period class.

```
ZonedDateTime nextMeeting = meeting.plus(Period.ofDays(7)); // OK
```

Table 5–5 ZonedDateTime Methods

Method	Description
now, of, ofInstant	These static methods construct a ZonedDateTime from the current time, or from a year, month, day, hour, minute, second, nanosecond (or a LocalDate and LocalTime), and ZoneId, or from an Instant and ZoneId.
plusDays, plusWeeks, plusMonths, plusYears, plusHours, plusMinutes, plusSeconds, plusNanos	Adds a number of temporal units to this ZonedDateTime.
minusDays, minusWeeks, minusMonths, minusYears, minusHours, minusMinutes, minusSeconds, minusNanos	Subtracts a number of temporal units from this ZonedDateTime.
plus, minus	Adds or subtracts a Duration or Period.
withDayOfMonth, withDayOfYear, withMonth, withYear, withHour, withMinute, withSecond, withNano	Returns a new ZonedDateTime, with one temporal unit changed to the given value.
withZoneSameInstant, withZoneSameLocal	Returns a new ZonedDateTime in the given time zone, either representing the same instant or the same local time.
getDayOfMonth	Gets the day of the month (between 1 and 31).
getDayOfYear	Gets the day of the year (between 1 and 366).
getDayOfWeek	Gets the day of the week, returning a value of the DayOfWeek enumeration.
getMonth, getMonthValue	Gets the month as a value of the Month enumeration, or as a number between 1 and 12.
getYear	Gets the year, between –999,999,999 and 999,999,999.
getHour, getMinute, getSecond, getNano	Gets the hour, minute, second, or nanosecond of this ZonedDateTime.

(Continues)

Table 5–5 ZonedDateTime Methods *(Continued)*

Method	Description
getOffset	Gets the offset from UTC, as a ZoneOffset instance. Offsets can vary from –12:00 to +14:00. Some time zones have fractional offsets. Offsets change with daylight savings time.
toLocalDate, toLocalTime, toInstant	Yields the local date or local time, or the corresponding instant.
isBefore, isAfter	Compares this ZonedDateTime with another.

 CAUTION: There is also an OffsetDateTime class that represents times with an offset from UTC, but without time zone rules. That class is intended for specialized applications that specifically require the absence of those rules, such as certain network protocols. For human time, use ZonedDateTime.

5.6 Formatting and Parsing

The DateTimeFormatter class provides three kinds of formatters to print a date/time value:

- Predefined standard formatters (see Table 5–6)
- Locale-specific formatters
- Formatters with custom patterns

To use one of the standard formatters, simply call its format method:

```
String formatted = DateTimeFormatter.ISO_DATE_TIME.format(apollo11launch);
   // 1969-07-16T09:32:00-05:00[America/New_York]
```

The standard formatters are mostly intended for machine-readable time-stamps. To present dates and times to human readers, use a locale-specific formatter. There are four styles, SHORT, MEDIUM, LONG, and FULL, for both date and time—see Table 5–7.

The static methods ofLocalizedDate, ofLocalizedTime, and ofLocalizedDateTime create such a formatter. For example:

```
DateTimeFormatter formatter = DateTimeFormatter.ofLocalizedDateTime(FormatStyle.LONG);
String formatted = formatter.format(apollo11launch);
   // July 16, 1969 9:32:00 AM EDT
```

These methods use the default locale. To change to a different locale, simply use the withLocale method.

5.6 ■ Formatting and Parsing 113

```
formatted = formatter.withLocale(Locale.FRENCH).format(apollo11launch);
    // 16 juillet 1969 09:32:00 EDT
```

Table 5–6 Predefined Formatters

Formatter	Description	Example
BASIC_ISO_DATE	Year, month, day, zone offset without separators	19690716-0500
ISO_LOCAL_DATE, ISO_LOCAL_TIME, ISO_LOCAL_DATE_TIME	Separators -, :, T	1969-07-16, 09:32:00, 1969-07-16T09:32:00
ISO_OFFSET_DATE, ISO_OFFSET_TIME, ISO_OFFSET_DATE_TIME	Like ISO_LOCAL_XXX, but with zone offset	1969-07-16-05:00, 09:32:00-05:00, 1969-07-16T09:32:00-05:00
ISO_ZONED_DATE_TIME	With zone offset and zone ID	1969-07-16T09:32:00-05:00[America/New_York]
ISO_INSTANT	In UTC, denoted by the Z zone ID	1969-07-16T14:32:00Z
ISO_DATE, ISO_TIME, ISO_DATE_TIME	Like ISO_OFFSET_DATE, ISO_OFFSET_TIME, ISO_ZONED_DATE_TIME, but the zone information is optional	1969-07-16-05:00, 09:32:00-05:00, 1969-07-16T09:32:00-05:00[America/New_York]
ISO_ORDINAL_DATE	The year and day of year, for LocalDate	1969-197
ISO_WEEK_DATE	The year, week, and day of week, for LocalDate	1969-W29-3
RFC_1123_DATE_TIME	The standard for email timestamps, codified in RFC 822 and updated to four digits for the year in RFC 1123	Wed, 16 Jul 1969 09:32:00 -0500

Table 5–7 Locale-Specific Formatting Styles

Style	Date	Time
SHORT	7/16/69	9:32 AM
MEDIUM	Jul 16, 1969	9:32:00 AM
LONG	July 16, 1969	9:32:00 AM EDT
FULL	Wednesday, July 16, 1969	9:32:00 AM EDT

 NOTE: The java.time.format.DateTimeFormatter class is intended as a re-placement for java.util.DateFormat. If you need an instance of the latter for backwards compatibility, call formatter.toFormat().

Finally, you can roll your own date format by specifying a pattern. For example,

```
formatter = DateTimeFormatter.ofPattern("E yyyy-MM-dd HH:mm");
```

formats a date in the form Wed 1969-07-16 09:32. Each letter denotes a different time field, and the number of times the letter is repeated selects a particular format, according to rules that are arcane and seem to have organically grown over time. Table 5–8 shows the most useful pattern elements.

Table 5–8 Commonly Used Formatting Symbols for Date/Time Formats

ChronoField or Purpose	Examples
ERA	G: AD, GGGG: Anno Domini, GGGGG: A
YEAR_OF_ERA	yy: 69, yyyy: 1969
MONTH_OF_YEAR	M: 7, MM: 07, MMM: Jul, MMMM: July, MMMMM: J
DAY_OF_MONTH	d: 6, dd: 06
DAY_OF_WEEK	e: 3, E: Wed, EEEE: Wednesday, EEEEE: W
HOUR_OF_DAY	H: 9, HH: 09
CLOCK_HOUR_OF_AM_PM	K: 9, KK: 09
AMPM_OF_DAY	a: AM
MINUTE_OF_HOUR	mm: 02

Table 5–8 Commonly Used Formatting Symbols for Date/Time Formats *(Continued)*

ChronoField or Purpose	Examples
SECOND_OF_MINUTE	ss: 00
NANO_OF_SECOND	nnnnnn: 000000
Time zone ID	VV: America/New_York
Time zone name	z: EDT, zzzz: Eastern Daylight Time
Zone offset	x: -04, xx: -0400, xxx: -04:00, XXX: same, but use Z for zero
Localized zone offset	O: GMT-4, OOOO: GMT-04:00

To parse a date/time value from a string, use one of the static parse methods. For example,

```
LocalDate churchsBirthday = LocalDate.parse("1903-06-14");
ZonedDateTime apollo11launch =
    ZonedDateTime.parse("1969-07-16 03:32:00-0400",
        DateTimeFormatter.ofPattern("yyyy-MM-dd HH:mm:ssxx"));
```

The first call uses the standard ISO_LOCAL_DATE formatter, the second one a custom formatter.

5.7 Interoperating with Legacy Code

As a brand-new creation, the Java Date and Time API will have to interoperate with existing classes, in particular, the ubiquitous java.util.Date, java.util. GregorianCalendar, and java.sql.Date/Time/Timestamp.

The Instant class is a close analog to java.util.Date. In Java 8, that class has two added methods: the toInstant method that converts a Date to an Instant, and the static from method that converts in the other direction.

Similarly, ZonedDateTime is a close analog to java.util.GregorianCalendar, and that class has gained conversion methods in Java 8. The toZonedDateTime method converts a GregorianCalendar to a ZonedDateTime, and the static from method does the opposite conversion.

Another set of conversions is available for the date and time classes in the java.sql package. You can also pass a DateTimeFormatter to legacy code that uses java.text.Format. Table 5–9 summarizes these conversions.

Table 5–9 Conversions between java.time Classes and Legacy Classes

Classes	To Legacy Class	From Legacy Class
Instant ↔ java.util.Date	Date.from(instant)	date.toInstant()
ZonedDateTime ↔ java.util.GregorianCalendar	GregorianCalendar. from(zonedDateTime)	cal.toZonedDateTime()
Instant ↔ java.sql.Timestamp	TimeStamp.from(instant)	timestamp.toInstant()
LocalDateTime ↔ java.sql.Timestamp	Timestamp. valueOf(localDateTime)	timeStamp.toLocalDateTime()
LocalDate ↔ java.sql.Date	Date.valueOf(localDate)	date.toLocalDate()
LocalTime ↔ java.sql.Time	Time.valueOf(localTime)	time.toLocalTime()
DateTimeFormatter → java.text.DateFormat	formatter.toFormat()	None
java.util.TimeZone → ZoneId	Timezone.getTimeZone(id)	timeZone.toZoneId()
java.nio.file.attribute.FileTime → Instant	FileTime.from(instant)	fileTime.toInstant()

Exercises

1. Compute Programmer's Day without using plusDays.

2. What happens when you add one year to LocalDate.of(2000, 2, 29)? Four years? Four times one year?

3. Implement a method next that takes a Predicate<LocalDate> and returns an adjuster yielding the next date fulfilling the predicate. For example,

   ```
   today.with(next(w -> getDayOfWeek().getValue() < 6))
   ```

   computes the next workday.

4. Write an equivalent of the Unix cal program that displays a calendar for a month. For example, java Cal 3 2013 should display

```
            1  2  3
   4  5  6  7  8  9 10
  11 12 13 14 15 16 17
  18 19 20 21 22 23 24
  25 26 27 28 29 30 31
```

indicating that March 1 is a Friday. (Show the weekend at the end of the week.)

5. Write a program that prints how many days you have been alive.

6. List all Friday the 13th in the twentieth century.

7. Implement a TimeInterval class that represents an interval of time, suitable for calendar events (such as a meeting on a given date from 10:00 to 11:00). Provide a method to check whether two intervals overlap.

8. Obtain the offsets of today's date in all supported time zones for the current time instant, turning ZoneId.getAvailableZoneIds into a stream and using stream operations.

9. Again using stream operations, find all time zones whose offsets aren't full hours.

10. Your flight from Los Angeles to Frankfurt leaves at 3:05 pm local time and takes 10 hours and 50 minutes. When does it arrive? Write a program that can handle calculations like this.

11. Your return flight leaves Frankfurt at 14:05 and arrives in Los Angeles at 16:40. How long is the flight? Write a program that can handle calculations like this.

12. Write a program that solves the problem described at the beginning of Section 5.5, "Zoned Time," on page 109. Read a set of appointments in different time zones and alert the user which ones are due within the next hour in local time.

Concurrency Enhancements

Chapter 6

Concurrent programming is hard, and it is harder without the right tools. Early Java releases had minimal support for concurrency, and programmers busily created code with deadlocks and race conditions. The robust `java.util.concurrent` package didn't appear until Java 5. That package gives us threadsafe collections and thread pools, allowing many application programmers to write concurrent programs without using locks or starting threads. Unfortunately, `java.util.concurrent` is a mix of useful utilities for the application programmer and power tools for library authors, without much effort to separate the two. In this chapter, we focus squarely on the needs of the application programmer.

The key points of this chapter are:

* Updating atomic variables has become simpler with the `updateAndGet`/`accumulateAndGet` methods.

* `LongAccumulator`/`DoubleAccumulator` are more efficient than `AtomicLong`/`AtomicDouble` under high contention.

* Updating entries in a `ConcurrentHashMap` has become simpler with the `compute` and `merge` methods.

* `ConcurrentHashMap` now has bulk operations `search`, `reduce`, `forEach`, with variants operating on keys, values, keys and values, and entries.

- A set view lets you use a ConcurrentHashMap as a Set.
- The Arrays class has methods for parallel sorting, filling, and prefix operations.
- Completable futures let you compose asynchronous operations.

6.1 Atomic Values

Since Java 5, the java.util.concurrent.atomic package provided classes for lock-free mutation of variables. For example, you can safely generate a sequence of numbers like this:

```
public static AtomicLong nextNumber = new AtomicLong();
// In some thread ...
long id = nextNumber.incrementAndGet();
```

The incrementAndGet method atomically increments the AtomicLong and returns the post-increment value. That is, the operations of getting the value, adding 1, setting it, and producing the new value cannot be interrupted. It is guaranteed that the correct value is computed and returned, even if multiple threads access the same instance concurrently.

There are methods for atomically setting, adding, and subtracting values, but if you want to make a more complex update, you have to use the compareAndSet method. For example, suppose you want to keep track of the largest value that is observed by different threads. The following won't work:

```
public static AtomicLong largest = new AtomicLong();
// In some thread ...
largest.set(Math.max(largest.get(), observed)); // Error—race condition!
```

This update is not atomic. Instead, compute the new value and use compareAndSet in a loop:

```
do {
   oldValue = largest.get();
   newValue = Math.max(oldValue, observed);
} while (!largest.compareAndSet(oldValue, newValue));
```

If another thread is also updating largest, it is possible that it has beat this thread to it. Then compareAndSet will return false without setting the new value. In that case, the loop tries again, reading the updated value and trying to change it. Eventually, it will succeed replacing the existing value with the new one. This sounds tedious, but the compareAndSet method maps to a processor operation that is faster than using a lock.

In Java 8, you don't have to write the loop boilerplate any more. Instead, you provide a lambda expression for updating the variable, and the update is done for you. In our example, we can call

```
largest.updateAndGet(x -> Math.max(x, observed));
```

or

```
largest.accumulateAndGet(observed, Math::max);
```

The `accumulateAndGet` method takes a binary operator that is used to combine the atomic value and the supplied argument.

There are also methods `getAndUpdate` and `getAndAccumulate` that return the old value.

 NOTE: These methods are also provided for the classes `AtomicInteger`, `AtomicIntegerArray`, `AtomicIntegerFieldUpdater`, `AtomicLongArray`, `AtomicLongFieldUpdater`, `AtomicReference`, `AtomicReferenceArray`, and `AtomicReferenceFieldUpdater`.

When you have a very large number of threads accessing the same atomic values, performance suffers because the optimistic updates require too many retries. Java 8 provides classes `LongAdder` and `LongAccumulator` to solve this problem. A `LongAdder` is composed of multiple variables whose collective sum is the current value. Multiple threads can update different summands, and new summands are automatically provided when the number of threads increases. This is efficient in the common situation where the value of the sum is not needed until after all work has been done. The performance improvement can be substantial—see Exercise 3.

If you anticipate high contention, you should simply use a `LongAdder` instead of an `AtomicLong`. The method names are slightly different. Call `increment` to increment a counter or `add` to add a quantity, and `sum` to retrieve the total.

```
final LongAdder adder = new LongAdder();
for (...)
  pool.submit(() -> {
    while (...) {
      ...
      if (...) adder.increment();
    }
  });
...
long total = adder.sum();
```

NOTE: Of course, the increment method does *not* return the old value. Doing that would undo the efficiency gain of splitting the sum into multiple summands.

The LongAccumulator generalizes this idea to an arbitrary accumulation operation. In the constructor, you provide the operation, as well as its neutral element. To incorporate new values, call accumulate. Call get to obtain the current value. The following has the same effect as a LongAdder:

```
LongAccumulator adder = new LongAccumulator(Long::sum, 0);
// In some thread ...
adder.accumulate(value);
```

Internally, the accumulator has variables $a_1, a_2, \ldots, a_n$. Each variable is initialized with the neutral element (0 in our example).

When accumulate is called with value v, then one of them is atomically updated as $a_i = a_i \; op \; v$, where op is the accumulation operation written in infix form. In our example, a call to accumulate computes $a_i = a_i + v$ for some i.

The result of get is $a_1 \; op \; a_2 \; op \; \ldots \; op \; a_n$. In our example, that is the sum of the accumulators, $a_1 + a_2 + \ldots + a_n$.

If you choose a different operation, you can compute maximum or minimum (see Exercise 4). In general, the operation must be associative and commutative. That means that the final result must be independent of the order in which the intermediate values were combined.

There are also DoubleAdder and DoubleAccumulator that work in the same way, except with double values.

 NOTE: Another addition to Java 8 is the StampedLock class that can be used to implement optimistic reads. I don't recommend that application programmers use locks, but here is how it is done. You first call tryOptimisticRead, upon which you get a "stamp." Read your values and check whether the stamp is still valid (i.e., no other thread has obtained a write lock). If so, you can use the values. If not, get a read lock (which blocks any writers). Here is an example.

```
public class Vector {
   private int size;
   private Object[] elements;
   private StampedLock lock = new StampedLock();

   public Object get(int n) {
      long stamp = lock.tryOptimisticRead();
      Object[] currentElements = elements;
      int currentSize = size;
      if (!lock.validate(stamp)) { // Someone else had a write lock
         stamp = lock.readLock(); // Get a pessimistic lock
         currentElements = elements;
         currentSize = size;
         lock.unlockRead(stamp);
      }
      return n < currentSize ? currentElements[n] : null;
   }
   ...
}
```

6.2 ConcurrentHashMap Improvements

A classic programmer's saying is, "If you can only have one data structure, make it a hash table." Since Java 5, the ConcurrentHashMap has been a workhorse of concurrent programming. A ConcurrentHashMap is, of course, threadsafe—multiple threads can add and remove elements without damaging the internal structure. Moreover, it is quite efficient, allowing multiple threads to update different parts of the table concurrently without blocking each other.

 NOTE: Some applications use humongous concurrent hash maps, so large that the size method is insufficient because it returns an int. What is one to do with a map that has over two billion entries? Java 8 introduces a mappingCount method that returns the size as a long.

NOTE: A hash map keeps all entries with the same hash code in the same "bucket." Some applications use poor hash functions, and as a result all entries end up in a small number of buckets, severely degrading performance. Even generally reasonable hash functions, such as that of the String class, can be problematic. For example, an attacker can slow down a program by crafting a large number of strings that hash to the same value. As of Java 8, the concurrent hash map organizes the buckets as trees, not lists, when the key type implements Comparable, guaranteeing $O(\log(n))$ performance.

6.2.1 Updating Values

The original version of ConcurrentHashMap only had a few methods for atomic updates, which made for somewhat awkward programming. Suppose we want to count how often certain features are observed. As a simple example, suppose multiple threads encounter words, and we want to count their frequencies.

Can we use a ConcurrentHashMap<String, Long>? Consider the code for incrementing a count. Obviously, the following is not threadsafe:

```
Long oldValue = map.get(word);
Long newValue = oldValue == null ? 1 : oldValue + 1;
map.put(word, newValue); // Error—might not replace oldValue
```

Another thread might be updating the exact same count at the same time.

 NOTE: Some programmers are surprised that a supposedly threadsafe data structure permits operations that are not threadsafe. But there are two entirely different considerations. If multiple threads modify a plain HashMap, they can destroy the internal structure (an array of linked lists). Some of the links may go missing, or even go in circles, rendering the data structure unusable. That will never happen with a ConcurrentHashMap. In the example above, the code for get and put will never corrupt the data structure. But, since the sequence of operations is not atomic, the result is not predictable.

One remedy is to use the replace operation, replacing a known old value with a new one, just as you have seen in the preceding section:

```
do {
    oldValue = map.get(word);
    newValue = oldValue == null ? 1 : oldValue + 1;
} while (!map.replace(word, oldValue, newValue));
```

Alternatively, you can use a ConcurrentHashMap<String, AtomicLong> or, with Java 8, a ConcurrentHashMap<String, LongAdder>. Then the update code is:

```
map.putIfAbsent(word, new LongAdder());
map.get(word).increment();
```

The first statement ensures that there is a LongAdder present that we can increment atomically.

Java 8 provides methods that make atomic updates more convenient. The compute method is called with a key and a function to compute the new value. That function receives the key and the associated value, or null if there is none, and it computes the new value. For example, here is how we can update a map of integer counters:

```
map.compute(word, (k, v) -> v == null ? 1 : v + 1);
```

 NOTE: You cannot have null values in a ConcurrentHashMap. There are many methods that use a null value as an indication that a given key is not present in the map.

There are also variants computeIfPresent and computeIfAbsent that only compute a new value when there is already an old one, or when there isn't yet one. A map of LongAdder counters can be updated with

```
map.computeIfAbsent(word, k -> new LongAdder()).increment();
```

That is almost like the call to putIfAbsent that you saw before, but the LongAdder constructor is only called when a new counter is actually needed.

You often need to do something special when a key is added for the first time. The merge method makes this particularly convenient. It has a parameter for the initial value that is used when the key is not yet present. Otherwise, the function that you supplied is called, combining the existing value and the initial value. (Unlike compute, the function does *not* process the key.)

```
map.merge(word, 1L, (existingValue, newValue) -> existingValue + newValue);
```

or, more simply,

```
map.merge(word, 1L, Long::sum);
```

It doesn't get more concise than that. See Exercise 5 for another compelling application of the merge method.

 NOTE: If the function that is passed to compute or merge returns null, the existing entry is removed from the map.

CAUTION: When you use compute or merge, keep in mind that the function that you supply should not do a lot of work. While that function runs, some other updates to the map may be blocked. Of course, that function should also not update other parts of the map.

6.2.2 Bulk Operations

Java 8 provides bulk operations on concurrent hash maps that can safely execute even while other threads operate on the map. The bulk operations traverse the map and operate on the elements they find as they go along. No effort is made to freeze a snapshot of the map in time. Unless you happen to know that the map is not being modified while a bulk operation runs, you should treat its result as an approximation of the map's state.

There are three kinds of operations:

- search applies a function to each key and/or value, until the function yields a non-null result. Then the search terminates and the function's result is returned.

- reduce combines all keys and/or values, using a provided accumulation function.

- forEach applies a function to all keys and/or values.

Each operation has four versions:

- searchKeys/reduceKeys/forEachKey: operates on keys.

- searchValues/reduceValues/forEachValue: operates on values.

- search/reduce/forEach: operates on keys and values.

- searchEntries/reduceEntries/forEachEntry: operates on Map.Entry objects.

With each of the operations, you need to specify a *parallelism threshold*. If the map contains more elements than the threshold, the bulk operation is parallelized. If you want the bulk operation to run in a single thread, use a threshold of Long.MAX_VALUE. If you want the maximum number of threads to be made available for the bulk operation, use a threshold of 1.

Let's look at the search methods first. Here are the versions:

```
U searchKeys(long threshold, Function<? super K, ? extends U> f)
U searchValues(long threshold, Function<? super V, ? extends U> f)
U search(long threshold, BiFunction<? super K, ? super V,? extends U> f)
U searchEntries(long threshold, Function<Map.Entry<K, V>, ? extends U> f)
```

For example, suppose we want to find the first word that occurs more than 1,000 times. We need to search keys and values:

```
String result = map.search(threshold, (k, v) -> v > 1000 ? k : null);
```

Then result is set to the first match, or to null if the search function returns null for all inputs.

The forEach methods have two variants. The first one simply applies a *consumer* function for each map entry, for example

```
map.forEach(threshold,
    (k, v) -> System.out.println(k + " -> " + v));
```

The second variant takes an additional *transformer* function, which is applied first, and its result is passed to the consumer:

```
map.forEach(threshold,
    (k, v) -> k + " -> " + v, // Transformer
System.out::println); // Consumer
```

The transformer can be used as a filter. Whenever the transformer returns null, the value is silently skipped. For example, here we only print the entries with large values:

```
map.forEach(threshold,
    (k, v) -> v > 1000 ? k + " -> " + v : null, // Filter and transformer
System.out::println); // The nulls are not passed to the consumer
```

The reduce operations combine their inputs with an accumulation function. For example, here is how you can compute the sum of all values.

```
Long sum = map.reduceValues(threshold, Long::sum);
```

As with forEach, you can also supply a transformer function. Here we compute the length of the longest key:

```
Integer maxlength = map.reduceKeys(threshold,
    String::length, // Transformer
Integer::max); // Accumulator
```

The transformer can act as a filter, by returning null to exclude unwanted inputs. Here, we count how many entries have value > 1000:

```
Long count = map.reduceValues(threshold,
    v -> v > 1000 ? 1L : null,
Long::sum);
```

 NOTE: If the map is empty, or all entries have been filtered out, the reduce operation returns null. If there is only one element, its transformation is returned, and the accumulator is not applied.

There are specializations for int, long, and double outputs with suffix ToInt, ToLong, and ToDouble. You need to transform the input to a primitive value and specify a default value and an accumulator function. The default value is returned when the map is empty.

```
long sum = map.reduceValuesToLong(threshold,
    Long::longValue, // Transformer to primitive type
    0, // Default value for empty map
    Long::sum); // Primitive type accumulator
```

 CAUTION: These specializations act differently from the object versions where there is only one element to be considered. Instead of returning the transformed element, it is accumulated with the default. Therefore, the default must be the neutral element of the accumulator.

6.2.3 Set Views

Suppose you want a large, threadsafe set instead of a map. There is no ConcurrentHashSet class, and you know better than trying to create your own. Of course, you can use a ConcurrentHashMap with bogus values, but then you get a map, not a set, and you can't apply operations of the Set interface.

The static newKeySet method yields a Set<K> that is actually a wrapper around a ConcurrentHashMap<K, Boolean>. (All map values are Boolean.TRUE, but you don't actually care since you just use it as a set.)

```
Set<String> words = ConcurrentHashMap.<String>newKeySet();
```

Of course, if you have an existing map, the keySet method yields the set of keys. That set is mutable. If you remove the set's elements, the keys (and their values) are removed from the map. But it doesn't make sense to add elements to the key set, because there would be no corresponding values to add. Java 8 adds a second keySet method to ConcurrentHashMap, with a default value, to be used when adding elements to the set:

```
Set<String> words = map.keySet(1L);
words.add("Java");
```

If "Java" wasn't already present in words, it now has a value of one.

6.3 Parallel Array Operations

The Arrays class now has a number of parallelized operations. The static Arrays.parallelSort method can sort an array of primitive values or objects. For example,

```
String contents = new String(Files.readAllBytes(
    Paths.get("alice.txt")), StandardCharsets.UTF_8); // Read file into string
String[] words = contents.split("[\\P{L}]+"); // Split along nonletters
Arrays.parallelSort(words);
```

When you sort objects, you can supply a Comparator. With all methods, you can supply the bounds of a range, such as

```
Arrays.parallelSort(values, values.length / 2, values.length); // Sort the upper half
```

 NOTE: At first glance, it seems a bit odd that these methods have parallel in their name, since the user shouldn't care how the sorting happens. However, the API designers wanted to make it clear that the sorting is parallelized. That way, users are on notice to avoid comparators with side effect.

The parallelSetAll method fills an array with values that are computed from a function. The function receives the element index and computes the value at that location.

```
Arrays.parallelSetAll(values, i -> i % 10);
    // Fills values with 0 1 2 3 4 5 6 7 8 9 0 1 2 ...
```

Clearly, this operation benefits from being parallelized. There are versions for all primitive type arrays and for object arrays.

Finally, there is a parallelPrefix method that replaces each array element with the accumulation of the prefix for a given associative operation. Huh? Here is an example. Consider the array [1, 2, 3, 4, ...] and the × operation. After executing Arrays.parallelPrefix(values, (x, y) -> x * y), the array contains

$$[1, 1 \times 2, 1 \times 2 \times 3, 1 \times 2 \times 3 \times 4, ...]$$

Perhaps surprisingly, this computation can be parallelized. First, join neighboring elements, as indicated here:

$$[1, 1 \times 2, 3, 3 \times 4, 5, 5 \times 6, 7, 7 \times 8]$$

The gray values are left alone. Clearly, one can make this computation in parallel in separate regions of the array. In the next step, update the indicated elements by multiplying them with elements that are one or two positions below:

$$[1, 1 \times 2, 1 \times 2 \times 3, 1 \times 2 \times 3 \times 4, 5, 5 \times 6, 5 \times 6 \times 7, 5 \times 6 \times 7 \times 8]$$

This can again be done in parallel. After $\log(n)$ steps, the process is complete. This is a win over the straightforward linear computation if sufficient processors are available. On special-purpose hardware, this algorithm is commonly used, and users of such hardware are quite ingenious in adapting it to a variety of problems. Exercise 9 gives a simple example.

6.4 Completable Futures

The java.util.concurrent library provides a Future<T> interface to denote a value of type T that will be available at some point in the future. However, up to now, futures were rather limited. In the following sections, you will see how *completable futures* make it possible to compose asynchronous operations.

6.4.1 Futures

Here is a quick refresher on futures. Consider a method

```
public Future<String> readPage(URL url)
```

The method reads a web page in a separate thread, which is going to take a while. When you call

```
Future<String> contents = readPage(url);
```

the method returns right away, and you hold in your hands a Future<String>. Now suppose we want to extract all URLs from the page in order to build a web crawler. We have a class Parser with a method

```
public static List<URL> getLinks(String page)
```

How can we apply that method to the future object? Unfortunately, there is only one way. First, call the get method on the future to get its value when it becomes available. Then, process the result:

```
String page = contents.get();
List<URL> links = Parser.getLinks(page);
```

But the call to get is a blocking call. We are really no better off than with a method public String readPage(URL url) that blocks until the result is available.

Now in fairness, there has been some support for futures in java.util.concurrent, but an essential piece was missing. There was no easy way of saying: "When the result becomes available, here is how to process it." This is the crucial feature that the new CompletableFuture<T> class provides.

6.4.2 Composing Futures

Let's change the readPage method so that it returns a CompletableFuture<String>. Unlike a plain Future, a CompletableFuture has a method thenApply to which you can pass the post-processing function.

```
CompletableFuture<String> contents = readPage(url);
CompletableFuture<List<URL>> links = contents.thenApply(Parser::getLinks);
```

The thenApply method doesn't block either. It returns another future. When the first future has completed, its result is fed to the getLinks method, and the return value of that method becomes the final result.

This *composability* is the key aspect of the CompletableFuture class. Composing future actions solves a serious problem in programming asynchronous applications. The traditional approach for dealing with nonblocking calls is to use event handlers. The programmer registers a handler for the next action after completion. Of course, if the next action is also asynchronous, then the next action after that is in a different event handler. Even though the programmer thinks in terms of "first do step 1, then step 2, then step 3," the program logic becomes dispersed in different places. It gets worse when one has to add error handling. Suppose step 2 is "the user logs in"; then we may need to repeat that step since the user can mistype the credentials. Trying to implement such a control flow in a set of event handlers, or to understand it once it has been implemented, is challenging.

With completable futures, you just specify what you want to have done, and in which order. It won't all happen right away, of course, but what is important is that all the code is in one place.

6.4.3 The Composition Pipeline

In Chapter 2, you saw how a stream pipeline starts with stream creation, then goes through one or more transformations, and finishes with a terminal operation. The same is true for a pipeline of futures.

Start out by generating a CompletableFuture, usually with the static method supplyAsync. That method requires a Supplier<T>, that is, a function with no parameters yielding a T. The function is called on a separate thread. In our example, we can start out the pipeline with

```
CompletableFuture<String> contents
    = CompletableFuture.supplyAsync(() -> blockingReadPage(url));
```

There is also a static runAsync method that takes a Runnable, yielding a CompletableFuture<Void>. This is useful if you simply want to schedule one action after another, without passing data between them.

 NOTE: All methods ending in Async have two variants. One of them runs the provided action on the common ForkJoinPool. The other has a parameter of type java.util.concurrent.Executor, and it uses the given executor to run the action.

Next, you can call thenApply or thenApplyAsync to run another action, either in the same thread or another. With either method, you supply a function and you get a CompletableFuture<U>, where U is the return type of the function. For example, here is a two-stage pipeline for reading and processing the web page:

```
CompletableFuture<List<URL>> links
    = CompletableFuture.supplyAsync(() -> blockingReadPage(url))
        .thenApply(Parser::getLinks);
```

You can have additional processing steps. Eventually, you'll be done, and you will need to save the results somewhere. Here, we just print the result.

```
CompletableFuture<Void> links
    = CompletableFuture.supplyAsync(() -> blockingReadPage(url))
        .thenApply(Parser::getLinks)
        .thenAccept(System.out::println);
```

The thenAccept method takes a Consumer—that is, a function with return type void.

Ideally, you would never call get on a future. The last step in the pipeline simply deposits the result where it belongs.

 NOTE: You don't explicitly start the computation. The static supplyAsync method starts it automatically, and the other methods cause it to be continued.

6.4.4 Composing Asynchronous Operations

There is a large number of methods for working with completable futures. Let us first look at those that deal with a single future (see Table 6–1). For each method shown, there are also two Async variants that I don't show. As noted in the preceding section, one of them uses the common ForkJoinPool, and the other has an Executor parameter. In the table, I use a shorthand notation for the ponderous functional interfaces, writing T -> U instead of Function<? super T, U>. These aren't actual Java types, of course.

You have already seen the thenApply method. The calls

```
CompletableFuture<U> future.thenApply(f);
CompletableFuture<U> future.thenApplyAsync(f);
```

return a future that applies f to the result of future when it is available. The second call runs f in yet another thread.

The thenCompose method, instead of taking a function T -> U, takes a function T -> CompletableFuture<U>. That sounds rather abstract, but it can be quite natural. Consider the action of reading a web page from a given URL. Instead of supplying a method

```
public String blockingReadPage(URL url)
```

Table 6-1 Adding an Action to a CompletableFuture<T> Object

Method	Parameter	Description
thenApply	T -> U	Apply a function to the result.
thenCompose	T -> CompletableFuture<U>	Invoke the function on the result and execute the returned future.
handle	(T, Throwable) -> U	Process the result or error.
thenAccept	T -> void	Like thenApply, but with void result.
whenComplete	(T, Throwable) -> void	Like handle, but with void result.
thenRun	Runnable	Execute the Runnable with void result.

it is more elegant to have that method return a future:

```
public CompletableFuture<String> readPage(URL url)
```

Now, suppose we have another method that gets the URL from user input, perhaps from a dialog that won't reveal the answer until the user has clicked the OK button. That, too, is an event in the future:

```
public CompletableFuture<URL> getURLInput(String prompt)
```

Here we have two functions T -> CompletableFuture<U> and U -> CompletableFuture<V>. Clearly, they compose to a function T -> CompletableFuture<V> by calling the second function when the first one has completed. That is exactly what thenCompose does.

The third method in Table 6–1 focuses on a different aspect that I have ignored so far: failure. When an exception is thrown in a CompletableFuture, it is captured and wrapped in an unchecked ExecutionException when the get method is called. But perhaps get is never called. In order to handle an exception, use the handle method. The supplied function is called with the result (or null if none) and the exception (or null if none), and it gets to make sense of the situation.

The remaining methods have void result and are usually used at the end of a processing pipeline.

Now let us turn to methods that combine multiple futures (see Table 6–2).

The first three methods run a CompletableFuture<T> and a CompletableFuture<U> action in parallel and combine the results.

The next three methods run two CompletableFuture<T> actions in parallel. As soon as one of them finishes, its result is passed on, and the other result is ignored.

Finally, the static allOf and anyOf methods take a variable number of completable futures and yield a CompletableFuture<Void> that completes when all of them, or any one of them, completes. No results are propagated.

Table 6–2 Combining Multiple Composition Objects

Method	Parameters	Description
thenCombine	CompletableFuture<U>, (T, U) -> V	Execute both and combine the results with the given function.
thenAcceptBoth	CompletableFuture<U>, (T, U) -> void	Like thenCombine, but with void result.
runAfterBoth	CompletableFuture<?>, Runnable	Execute the runnable after both complete.
applyToEither	CompletableFuture<T>, T -> V	When a result is available from one or the other, pass it to the given function.
acceptEither	CompletableFuture<T>, T -> void	Like applyToEither, but with void result.
runAfterEither	CompletableFuture<?>, Runnable	Execute the runnable after one or the other completes.
static allOf	CompletableFuture<?>...	Complete with void result after all given futures complete.
static anyOf	CompletableFuture<?>...	Complete with void result after any of the given futures completes.

 NOTE: Technically speaking, the methods in this section accept parameters of type CompletionStage, not CompletableFuture. That is an interface type with almost forty abstract methods, currently implemented only by CompletableFuture. Most programmers wouldn't casually implement that interface, so I don't dwell on the distinction.

Exercises

1. Write a program that keeps track of the longest string that is observed by a number of threads. Use an AtomicReference and an appropriate accumulator.

2. Does a LongAdder help with yielding a sequence of increasing IDs? Why or why not?

3. Generate 1,000 threads, each of which increments a counter 100,000 times. Compare the performance of using AtomicLong versus LongAdder.

4. Use a `LongAccumulator` to compute the maximum or minimum of the accumulated elements.

5. Write an application in which multiple threads read all words from a collection of files. Use a `ConcurrentHashMap<String, Set<File>>` to track in which files each word occurs. Use the `merge` method to update the map.

6. Repeat the preceding exercise, but use `computeIfAbsent` instead. What is the advantage of this approach?

7. In a `ConcurrentHashMap<String, Long>`, find the key with maximum value (breaking ties arbitrarily). Hint: `reduceEntries`.

8. How large does an array have to be for `Arrays.parallelSort` to be faster than `Arrays.sort` on your computer?

9. You can use the `parallelPrefix` method to parallelize the computation of Fibonacci numbers. We use the fact that the nth Fibonacci number is the top left coefficient of F^n, where $F = \left(\begin{smallmatrix} 1 & 1 \\ 1 & 0 \end{smallmatrix}\right)$. Make an array filled with 2×2 matrices. Define a `Matrix` class with a multiplication method, use `parallelSetAll` to make an array of matrices, and use `parallelPrefix` to multiply them.

10. Write a program that asks the user for a URL, then reads the web page at that URL, and then displays all the links. Use a `CompletableFuture` for each stage. Don't call `get`. To prevent your program from terminating prematurely, call

    ```
    ForkJoinPool.commonPool().awaitQuiescence(10, TimeUnit.SECONDS);
    ```

11. Write a method

    ```
    public static <T> CompletableFuture<T> repeat(
        Supplier<T> action, Predicate<T> until)
    ```

    that asynchronously repeats the action until it produces a value that is accepted by the `until` function, which should also run asynchronously. Test with a function that reads a `java.net.PasswordAuthentication` from the console, and a function that simulates a validity check by sleeping for a second and then checking that the password is `"secret"`. Hint: Use recursion.

The Nashorn JavaScript Engine

Topics in This Chapter

Chapter 7

For many years, Java bundled the Rhino JavaScript interpreter, an open source JavaScript interpreter written in Java. It is called Rhino because a well-regarded JavaScript book has the image of a rhinoceros on its cover. Rhino works just fine, but it isn't particularly fast. Oracle's engineers realized that they could build a much more efficient JavaScript interpreter using the new JVM instructions designed for dynamic languages. Thus, the Nashorn project was born. Nashorn is the German word for rhinoceros—literally, nose-horn. (You get extra karma for pronouncing it nas-horn, not na-shorn.) Nashorn is very fast, and it lets you integrate Java with JavaScript on a highly performant virtual machine. It is also incredibly compliant with the ECMAScript standard for JavaScript. If you are thinking of giving your users the ability to script your application, or if you are intrigued by the ease of use of reactive programming environments such as node.js, check out Nashorn in Java 8. Not only do you get the benefits of a reasonably well-designed scripting language (i.e., JavaScript), but you have the full power of the JVM behind it.

The key points of this chapter are:

- Nashorn is the successor to the Rhino JavaScript interpreter, with greater performance and fidelity to the JavaScript standard.

- Nashorn is a pleasant environment for experimenting with the Java API.

- You can run JavaScript through the jjs interpreter, or from Java via the scripting API.

- Use the predefined JavaScript objects for the most common packages, or the Java.type function to access any package.

- Beware of intricacies in the conversion of strings and numbers between JavaScript and Java.

- JavaScript offers a convenient syntax for working with Java lists and maps, as well as JavaBeans properties.

- You can convert JavaScript functions to Java interfaces in a way that is very similar to using lambda expressions.

- You can extend Java classes and implement Java interfaces in JavaScript, but there are limitations.

- Nashorn has good support for writing shell scripts in JavaScript.

- You can write JavaFX programs in JavaScript, but the integration is not as good as it might be.

7.1 Running Nashorn from the Command Line

Java 8 ships with a command-line tool called jjs. Simply launch it, and issue JavaScript commands.

```
$ jjs
jjs> 'Hello, World'
Hello, World
```

You get what's called a "read-eval-print" loop, or REPL, in the world of Lisp, Scala, and so on. Whenever you enter an expression, its value is printed.

```
jjs> 'Hello, World!'.length
13
```

 NOTE: As a reminder, in JavaScript, strings can be delimited by '...' or "...". In this chapter, I will use single quotes for JavaScript strings to give you a visual clue that the code is JavaScript, not Java.

You can define functions and call them:

```
jjs> function factorial(n) { return n <= 1 ? 1 : n * factorial(n - 1) }
function factorial(n) { return n <= 1 ? 1 : n * factorial(n - 1) }
jjs> factorial(10)
3628800
```

You can call Java methods:

```
var input = new java.util.Scanner(
    new java.net.URL('http://horstmann.com').openStream())
input.useDelimiter('$')
var contents = input.next()
```

Now, when you type contents, you see the contents of the web page.

Look how refreshing this is. You didn't have to worry about exceptions. You can make experiments dynamically. I wasn't quite sure whether I could read the entire contents by setting the delimiter to $, but I tried it out and it worked. And I didn't have to write public static void main. I didn't have to compile a thing. I didn't have to make a project in my IDE. The REPL is the easiest way to explore an API. It is a bit odd that one drives Java from JavaScript, but it is also convenient. Note how I didn't have to define the types for the input and contents variables.

 TIP: There are two annoyances that keep the JavaScript REPL from being as refreshing as its equivalent in Scala. The Scala REPL has command completion. When you press the Tab key, you get a list of possible completions of the current expression. Admittedly, that is a difficult trick to pull off for dynamically typed languages such as JavaScript. A more fundamental omission is command-line recall. Pressing the ↑ key should get you the previous command. If it doesn't, try installing rlwrap and run rlwrap jjs. Alternatively, you can run jjs inside Emacs. Don't worry—this won't hurt a bit. Start Emacs and hit M-x (i.e., Alt+x or Esc x) shell Enter, then type jjs. Type expressions as usual. Use M-p and M-n to recall the previous or next line, and the left and right arrow keys to move within a line. Edit a command, then press Enter to see it executed.

7.2 Running Nashorn from Java

In the preceding section, you saw one use case for Nashorn scripting: to experiment with Java APIs from the jjs REPL. Another use case is to allow users of your programs to run scripts. In the desktop world, this is quite common. For example, all Microsoft Office applications can be scripted with a language called VB Script that is a descendant of the Basic language. Quite a few people write such scripts, and this capability leads to a form of vendor lock. It is difficult to adopt an alternate office suite that won't run those scripts. If you want to lock in the users of your Java desktop or server app, you can provide the same capabilities.

Running a Nashorn script from Java uses the script engine mechanism that has been introduced in Java 6. You can use that mechanism to execute scripts in any

JVM language with a script engine, such as Groovy, JRuby, or Jython. There are also script engines for languages that run outside the JVM, such as PHP or Scheme.

To run a script, you need to get a ScriptEngine object. If the engine is registered, you can simply get it by name. Java 8 includes an engine with name "nashorn". Here is how to use it:

```
ScriptEngineManager manager = new ScriptEngineManager();
ScriptEngine engine = manager.getEngineByName("nashorn");
Object result = engine.eval("'Hello, World!'.length");
System.out.println(result);
```

You can also read a script from a Reader:

```
Object result = engine.eval(Files.newBufferedReader(path));
```

To make a Java object available to your scripts, use the put method of the ScriptEngine interface. For example, you can make a JavaFX stage visible, so that you can populate it using JavaScript code:

```
public void start(Stage stage) {
    engine.put("stage", stage);
    engine.eval(script); // Script code can access the object as stage
}
```

Instead of putting variables into the global scope, you can collect them in an object of type Bindings and pass that object to the eval method:

```
Bindings scope = engine.createBindings();
scope.put("stage", stage);
engine.eval(script, scope);
```

This is useful if a set of bindings should not persist for future calls to the eval method.

7.3 Invoking Methods

In the preceding section, you saw how the script engine can make Java objects accessible to JavaScript. You can then invoke methods on the provided variables. For example, if the Java code calls

```
engine.put("stage", stage);
```

then the JavaScript code can call

```
stage.setTitle('Hello')
```

In fact, you can also use the syntax

```
stage.title = 'Hello'
```

Nashorn supports a convenient property syntax for getters and setters. If the expression stage.title occurs to the left of the = operator, it is translated to an invocation of the setTitle method. Otherwise it turns into a call stage.getTitle().

You can even use the JavaScript bracket notation to access properties:

```
stage['title'] = 'Hello'
```

Note that the argument of the [] operator is a string. In this context, that isn't useful, but you can call stage[str] with a string variable and thereby access arbitrary properties.

 NOTE: In JavaScript, semicolons at the end of a line are optional. Many JavaScript programmers put them in anyway, but in this chapter, I omit them so that you can easily distinguish between Java and JavaScript code snippets.

JavaScript has no concept of method overloading. There can be only one method with a given name, and it can have any number of parameters of any type. Nashorn attempts to pick the correct Java method, following the number and types of the parameters.

In almost all cases, there is only one Java method that matches the supplied parameters. If there is not, you can manually pick the correct method with the following rather strange syntax:

```
list['remove(Object)'](1)
```

Here, we specify the remove(Object) method that removes the Integer object 1 from the list. (There is also a remove(int) method that removes the object at position 1.)

7.4 Constructing Objects

When you want to construct objects in JavaScript (as opposed to having them handed to you from the script engine), you need to know how to access Java packages. There are two mechanisms.

There are global objects java, javax, javafx, com, org, and edu that yield package and class objects via the dot notation. For example,

```
var javaNetPackage = java.net // A JavaPackage object
var URL = java.net.URL // A JavaClass object
```

If you need to access a package that does not start with one of the above identifiers, you can find it in the Package object, such as Package.ch.cern.

Alternatively, call the Java.type function:

```
var URL = Java.type('java.net.URL')
```

This is a bit faster than java.net.URL, and you get better error checking. (If you make a spelling error such as java.net.Url, Nashorn will think it is a package.) But if you want speed and good error handling, you probably shouldn't be using a scripting language in the first place, so I will stick with the shorter form.

 NOTE: The Nashorn documentation suggests that class objects should be defined at the top of a script file, just like you place imports at the top of a Java file:

```
var URL = Java.type('java.net.URL')
var JMath = Java.type('java.lang.Math')
    // Avoids conflict with JavaScript Math object
```

Once you have a class object, you can call static methods:

```
JMath.floorMod(-3, 10)
```

To construct an object, pass the class object to the JavaScript new operator. Pass any constructor parameters in the usual way:

```
var URL = java.net.URL
var url = new URL('http://horstmann.com')
```

If you aren't concerned about efficiency, you can also call

```
var url = new java.net.URL('http://horstmann.com')
```

 CAUTION: If you use Java.type with new, you need an extra set of parentheses:

```
var url = new (Java.type('java.net.URL'))('http://horstmann.com')
```

If you need to specify an inner class, you can do so with the dot notation:

```
var entry = new java.util.AbstractMap.SimpleEntry('hello', 42)
```

Alternatively, if you use Java.type, use a $, like the JVM does:

```
var Entry = Java.type('java.util.AbstractMap$SimpleEntry')
```

7.5 Strings

Strings in Nashorn are, of course, JavaScript objects. For example, consider the call

```
'Hello'.slice(-2) // Yields 'lo'
```

Here, we call the JavaScript method slice. There is no such method in Java.

But the call

```
'Hello'.compareTo('World')
```

also works, even though in JavaScript there is no compareTo method. (You just use the < operator.)

In this case, the JavaScript string is converted to a Java string. In general, a JavaScript string is converted to a Java string whenever it is passed to a Java method.

Also note that *any* JavaScript object is converted to a string when it is passed to a Java method with a String parameter. Consider

```
var path = java.nio.file.Paths.get(/home/)
    // A JavaScript RegExp is converted to a Java String!
```

Here, /home/ is a regular expression. The Paths.get method wants a String, and it gets one, even though it makes no sense in this situation. One shouldn't blame Nashorn for this. It follows the general JavaScript behavior to turn anything into a string when a string is expected. The same conversion happens for numbers and Boolean values. For example, 'Hello'.slice('-2') is perfectly valid. The string '-2' is silently converted to the number –2. It is features such as this one that make programming in a dynamically typed language an exciting adventure.

7.6 Numbers

JavaScript has no explicit support for integers. Its Number type is the same as the Java double type. When a number is passed to Java code that expects an int or long, any fractional part is silently removed. For example, 'Hello'.slice(-2.99) is the same as 'Hello'.slice(-2).

For efficiency, Nashorn keeps computations as integers when possible, but that difference is generally transparent. Here is one situation when it is not:

```
var price = 10
java.lang.String.format('Price: %.2f', price)
    // Error: f format not valid for java.lang.Integer
```

The value of price happens to be an integer, and it is assigned to an Object since the format method has an Object... varargs parameter. Therefore, Nashorn produces a java.lang.Integer. That causes the format method to fail, since the f format is intended for floating-point numbers. In this case, you can force conversion to java.lang.Double by calling the Number function:

```
java.lang.String.format('Unit price: %.2f', Number(price))
```

7.7 Working with Arrays

To construct a Java array, first make a class object:

```
var intArray = Java.type('int[]')
var StringArray = Java.type('java.lang.String[]')
```

Then call the new operator and supply the length of the array:

```
var numbers = new intArray(10) // A primitive int[] array
var names = new StringArray(10) // An array of String references
```

Then use the bracket notation in the usual way:

```
numbers[0] = 42
print(numbers[0])
```

You get the length of the array as numbers.length. To iterate through all values of the names array, use

```
for each (var elem in names)
    Do something with elem
```

This is the equivalent of the enhanced for loop in Java. If you need the index values, use the following loop instead:

```
for (var i in names)
    Do something with i and names[i]
```

 CAUTION: Even though this loop looks just like the enhanced for loop in Java, it visits the index values. JavaScript arrays can be sparse. Suppose you initialize a JavaScript array as

```
var names = []
names[0] = 'Fred'
names[2] = 'Barney'
```

Then the loop for (var i in names) print(i) prints 0 and 2.

Java and JavaScript arrays are quite different. When you supply a JavaScript array where a Java array is expected, Nashorn will carry out the conversion. But sometimes, you need to help it along. Given a JavaScript array, use the Java.to method to obtain the equivalent Java array:

```
var javaNames = Java.to(names, StringArray) // An array of type String[]
```

Conversely, use Java.from to turn a Java array into a JavaScript array:

```
var jsNumbers = Java.from(numbers)
jsNumbers[-1] = 42
```

You need to use Java.to to resolve overload ambiguities. For example,

```
java.util.Arrays.toString([1, 2, 3])
```

is ambiguous since Nashorn can't decide whether to convert to an int[] or Object[] array. In that situation, call

```
java.util.Arrays.toString(Java.to([1, 2, 3], Java.type('int[]')))
```

or simply

```
java.util.Arrays.toString(Java.to([1, 2, 3], 'int[]'))
```

7.8 Lists and Maps

Nashorn provides "syntactic sugar" for Java lists and maps. You can use the bracket operator with any Java List to invoke the get and set methods:

```
var names = java.util.Arrays.asList('Fred', 'Wilma', 'Barney')
var first = names[0]
names[0] = 'Duke'
```

The bracket operator also works for Java maps:

```
var scores = new java.util.HashMap
scores['Fred'] = 10 // Calls scores.put('Fred', 10)
```

To visit all elements in the map, you can use the JavaScript for each loops:

```
for (var key in scores) ...
for each (var value in scores) ...
```

If you want to process keys and values together, simply iterate over the entry set:

```
for each (var e in scores.entrySet())
    Process e.key and e.value
```

 NOTE: The for each loop works for any Java class that implements the Iterable interface.

7.9 Lambdas

JavaScript has anonymous functions, such as

```
var square = function(x) { return x * x }
    // The right-hand side is an anonymous function
var result = square(2)
    // The () operator invokes the function
```

Syntactically, such an anonymous function is very similar to a Java lambda expression. Instead of an arrow after the parameter list, you have the keyword function.

You can use an anonymous function as a functional interface argument of a Java method, just like you could use a lambda expression in Java. For example,

```
java.util.Arrays.sort(words,
    function(a, b) { return java.lang.Integer.compare(a.length, b.length) })
    // Sorts the array by increasing length
```

Nashorn supports shorthand for functions whose body is a single expression. For such functions, you can omit the braces and the return keyword:

```
java.util.Arrays.sort(words,
    function(a, b) java.lang.Integer.compare(a.length, b.length))
```

Again, note the similarity with a Java lambda expression (a, b) -> Integer. compare(a.length, b.length).

 NOTE: That shorthand notation (called an "expression closure") is not part of the official JavaScript language standard (ECMAScript 5.1), but it is also supported by the Mozilla JavaScript implementation.

7.10 Extending Java Classes and Implementing Java Interfaces

To extend a Java class, or to implement a Java interface, use the Java.extend function. Supply the class object of the superclass or interface and a JavaScript object with the methods that you want to override or implement.

For example, here is an iterator that produces an infinite sequence of random numbers. We override two methods, next and hasNext. For each method, we provide an implementation as an anonymous JavaScript function:

```
var RandomIterator = Java.extend(java.util.Iterator, {
   next: function() Math.random(),
   hasNext: function() true
}) // RandomIterator is a class object
var iter = new RandomIterator() // Use it to construct an instance
```

> NOTE: When calling Java.extend, you can specify any number of super-interfaces as well as a superclass. Place all class objects before the object with the implemented methods.

Another Nashorn syntax extension lets you define anonymous subclasses of interfaces or abstract classes. When new *JavaClassObject* is followed by a JavaScript object, an object of the extended class is returned. For example,

```
var iter = new java.util.Iterator {
   next: function() Math.random(),
   hasNext: function() true
}
```

If the supertype is abstract and has only one abstract method, you don't even have to give the method name. Instead, pass the function as if it was a constructor parameter:

```
var task = new java.lang.Runnable(function() { print('Hello') })
   // task is an object of an anonymous class implementing Runnable
```

> CAUTION: When extending a *concrete* class, you cannot use that constructor syntax. For example, new java.lang.Thread(function() { print('Hello') }) calls a Thread constructor, in this case the constructor Thread(Runnable). The call to new returns an object of class Thread, not of a subclass of Thread.

If you want instance variables in your subclass, add them to the JavaScript object. For example, here is an iterator that produces ten random numbers:

```
var iter = new java.util.Iterator {
   count: 10,
   next: function() { this.count--; return Math.random() },
   hasNext: function() this.count > 0
}
```

Note that the JavaScript methods next and hasNext refer to the instance variable as this.count.

It is possible to invoke a superclass method when overriding a method, but it is quite finicky. The call Java.super(obj) yields an object on which you can invoke the superclass method of the class to which obj belongs, but you must have that object available. Here is a way to achieve that:

```
var arr = new (Java.extend(java.util.ArrayList)) {
    add: function(x) {
        print('Adding ' + x);
        return Java.super(arr).add(x)
    }
}
```

When you call arr.add('Fred'), a message is printed before the value is added to the array list. Note that the call Java.super(arr) requires the arr variable, which is being set to the value returned by new. Calling Java.super(this) does not work—that only gets the JavaScript object that defines the method, not the Java proxy. The Java.super mechanism is only useful for defining individual objects, not subclasses.

 NOTE: Instead of calling Java.super(arr).add(x), you can also use the syntax arr.super$add(x).

7.11 Exceptions

When a Java method throws an exception, you can catch it in JavaScript in the usual way:

```
try {
    var first = list.get(0)
    ...
} catch (e) {
    if (e instanceof java.lang.IndexOutOfBoundsException)
        print('list is empty')
}
```

Note that there is only one catch clause, unlike in Java where you can catch expressions by type. That, too, is in the spirit of dynamic languages where all type inquiry happens at runtime.

7.12 Shell Scripting

If you need to automate a repetitive task on your computer, chances are that you have put the commands in a *shell script*, a script that replays a set of OS-level commands. I have a directory ~/bin filled with dozens of shell scripts: to upload files to my web site, my blog, my photo storage, and to my publisher's FTP site; to convert images to blog size; to bulk-email my students; to back up my computer at two o'clock in the morning.

For me, these are bash scripts, but in the olden days when I used Windows they were batch files. So what is wrong with that? The problem comes once you have a need for branches and loops. For some reason, most implementors of command shells are terrible at programming language design. The way variables, branches, loops, and functions are implemented in bash is simply awful, and the batch language in Windows is even worse. I have a few bash scripts that started out modest but have over time accreted so much cruft that they are unmanageable. This is a common problem.

Why not just write these scripts in Java? Java is quite verbose. If you call external commands via Runtime.exec, you need to manage standard input/output/error streams. The Nashorn designers want you to consider JavaScript as an alternative. The syntax is comparatively lightweight, and Nashorn offers some conveniences that are specifically geared towards shell programmers.

7.12.1 Executing Shell Commands

To use the scripting extensions in Nashorn, run

```
jjs -scripting
```

or

```
jrunscript
```

Now you can execute shell commands by including them in backquotes, for example

```
`ls -al`
```

The standard output and standard error streams of the last command are captured in $OUT and $ERR. The exit code of the command is in $EXIT. (By convention, an exit code of zero means success, and non-zero codes describe error conditions.)

You can also capture the standard output by assigning the result of the backquoted command to a variable:

```
var output = `ls -al`
```

If you want to supply standard input for a command, use

```
$EXEC(command, input)
```

For example, this command passes the output of ls -al to grep -v class:

```
$EXEC('grep -v class', `ls -al`)
```

It's not quite as pretty as a pipe, but you can easily implement a pipe if you need it—see Exercise 6.

7.12.2 String Interpolation

Expressions inside ${...} are evaluated within doubly quoted and backquoted strings. This is called "string interpolation." For example,

```
var cmd = "javac -classpath ${classpath} ${mainclass}.java"
$EXEC(cmd)
```

or simply

```
`javac -classpath ${classpath} ${mainclass}.java`
```

injects the contents of the variables classpath and mainclass into the command.

You can use arbitrary expressions inside the ${...}:

```
var message = "The current time is ${java.time.Instant.now()}"
    // Sets message to a string such as The current time is 2013-10-12T21:48:58.545Z
```

As with the bash shell, string interpolation does not work inside singly quoted strings.

```
var message = 'The current time is ${java.time.Instant.now()}'
    // Sets message to The current time is ${java.time.Instant.now()}
```

Strings are also interpolated in "here documents"—inline documents in a script. These inline documents are useful when a command reads multiple lines from standard input and the script author doesn't want to put the input in a separate file. As an example, here is how you can feed commands to the GlassFish administration tool:

```
name='myapp'
dir='/opt/apps/myapp'
$EXEC("asadmin", <<END)
start-domain
start-database
deploy ${name} ${dir}
exit
END
```

The <<END construct means: "Insert the string that starts on the next line and is terminated by the line END." (Instead of END, you can use any identifier that doesn't appear inside the string.)

Note that the name and location of the application are interpolated.

String interpolation and here documents are only available in scripting mode.

7.12.3 Script Inputs

You can supply command-line arguments to a script. Since it is possible to include multiple script files on the jjs command line, you need to separate the script files and arguments with a --:

```
jjs script1.js script2.js -- arg1 arg2 arg3
```

> NOTE: That is a little ugly. If you have only one script file, you can instead run
>
> ```
> jrunscript -f script.js arg1 arg2 arg3
> ```

> TIP: The first line of a script can be a "shebang," the symbols #! followed by the location of the script interpreter. For example,
>
> ```
> #!/opt/java/bin/jjs
> ```
>
> or
>
> ```
> #!/opt/java/bin/jrunscript -f
> ```
>
> Then you can make the script file executable and simply run it as *path*/script.js.
>
> When a script starts with a shebang, scripting mode is automatically activated.

> CAUTION: If your script has arguments, and you use jjs in the shebang, script users will need to supply the --: *path*/script.js -- arg1 arg2 arg3. Users will not love you for that. Use jrunscript instead.

In the script file, you receive the command-line arguments in the arguments array:

```
var deployCommand = "deploy ${arguments[0]} ${arguments[1]}"
```

With jjs (but not with jrunscript), you can use $ARG instead of arguments. If you use that variable with string interpolation, you need two dollar signs:

```
var deployCommand = "deploy ${$ARG[0]} ${$ARG[1]}"
```

In your script, you can obtain the shell's environment variables through the ENV object:

```
var javaHome = $ENV.JAVA_HOME
```

In scripting mode, you can prompt the user for input with the readLine function:

```
var username = readLine('Username: ')
```

> CAUTION: To prompt for a password, call
>
> ```
> var password = java.lang.System.console().readPassword('Password: ')
> ```

Finally, to exit a script, use the exit function. You can supply an optional exit code.

```
if (username.length == 0) exit(1)
```

7.13 Nashorn and JavaFX

Nashorn provides a convenient way of launching JavaFX applications. Simply put the instructions that you would normally put into the start method of the Application subclass into the script. Use $STAGE for the Stage parameter. You don't even have to call show on the Stage object—that is done for you. For example, here is the "Hello" program from Chapter 4 in JavaScript:

```
var message = new javafx.scene.control.Label("Hello, JavaFX!");
message.font = new javafx.scene.text.Font(100);
$STAGE.scene = new javafx.scene.Scene(message);
$STAGE.title = "Hello";
```

Run the script with the -fx option, like this:

```
jjs -fx myJavaFxApp.js
```

That is all there is to it. A label with a message "Hello, JavaFX!" is displayed in a 100-point font in a window whose title is "Hello"—see Figure 7–1.

All the boilerplate is gone, and you have the convenient property notation, that is,

```
message.font = new Font(100)
```

instead of

```
message.setFont(new Font(100))
```

Figure 7–1   The Hello JavaFX application in JavaScript

NOTE: If you need to override the `init` or `stop` lifecycle methods of the `Application` class in addition to `start`, include the methods that you need in your script, at the top level. With the `-fx` option, you then get a subclass of `Application` with the script methods.

Now let us look at event handling. As you have seen in Chapter 4, most FX events are handled through listeners to FX properties. Here, the JavaScript story isn't so pretty. Recall that an FX property has two listener interfaces, `InvalidationListener` and `ChangeListener`, both added with the `addListener` method. In Java, you can call `addListener` with a lambda expression, and the compiler is able to figure out from the parameter types which of the two listeners to add. But in JavaScript, function parameters have no types. Suppose we have a slider to control the font size. We'd like to add a listener that updates the size when the slider value changes:

```
slider.valueProperty().addListener(function(property)
   message.font = new Font(slider.value))
   // Error—Nashorn can't determine which listener type to add
```

That doesn't work. Nashorn doesn't know whether you want to add an `InvalidationListener` or a `ChangeListener`, and it doesn't know that you don't actually care.

To fix this, you need to make the choice:

```
slider.valueProperty().addListener(
   new javafx.beans.InvalidationListener(function(property)
      message.font = new Font(slider.value)))
```

That's more heavyweight than the Java equivalent—not something one wants to see in a lightweight scripting language. There is nobody to blame for this, really. The JavaFX designers made the decision to overload the `addListener` method, which was perfectly reasonable in the context of Java 7 and mostly works with Java 8 lambda expressions. Compatibility with scripting languages was perhaps not their major concern, particularly since they had just abandoned another scripting language.

But it should be a cautionary tale. When you design a Java API, remember Atwood's law: "Any application that can be written in JavaScript will eventually be written in JavaScript." Design your API so that it can be accessed nicely from JavaScript.

And there is another sad aspect about the JavaFX support in Nashorn. Recall how in the olden days of JavaFX Script, it was easy to describe the layout of a scene like this:

```
Frame {
    title: "Hello"
    content: Label {
        text: "Hello, World!"
    }
}
```

Doesn't it almost look like JavaScript? Well, Nashorn/JavaFX developers, tear down that wall and turn it into JavaScript! Then we can write both the UI layout and event handling in JavaScript, and Atwood's law will be fulfilled.

Exercises

1. Pick some part of the Java API that you want to explore—for example, the ZonedDateTime class. Run some experiments in jjs: construct objects, call methods, and observe the returned values. Did you find it easier than writing test programs in Java?

2. Run jjs and, using the stream library, interactively work out a solution for the following problem: Print all unique long words (> 12 characters) from a file in sorted order. First read the words, then filter the long words, and so on. How does this interactive approach compare to your usual workflow?

3. Run jjs. Call

   ```
   var b = new java.math.BigInteger('12345678909876543321')
   ```

   Then display b (simply by typing b and Enter). What do you get? What is the value of b.mod(java.math.BigInteger.TEN)? Why is b displayed so strangely? How can you display the actual value of b?

4. Construct a nonliteral JavaScript string by extracting a substring from another string, and invoke the getClass method. What class do you get? Then pass the object to java.lang.String.class.cast. What happens? Why?

5. At the end of Section 7.10, "Extending Java Classes and Implementing Java Interfaces," on page 146, you saw how to extend ArrayList so that every call to add is logged. But that only worked for a single object. Write a JavaScript function that is a factory for such objects, so that one can generate any number of logging array lists.

6. Write a JavaScript function pipe that takes a sequence of shell commands and pipes the output of one to the input of the next, returning the final output. For example, pipe('find .', 'grep -v class', 'sort'). Simply call $EXEC repeatedly.

7. The solution of the preceding exercise is not quite as good as a Unix pipe because the second command only starts when the first one has finished. Remedy that by using the ProcessBuilder class.

8. Write a script that prints the values of all environment variables.

9. Write a script `nextYear.js` that obtains the age of the user and then prints `Next year, you will be ...`, adding 1 to the input. The age can be specified on the command line or the `AGE` environment variable. If neither are present, prompt the user.

10. Write a JavaFX program in JavaScript that reads data from a source of your choice and renders a pie chart. Was it easier or harder than developing the program in Java? Why?

Miscellaneous Goodies

Topics in This Chapter

Chapter 8

Java 8 is a big release with important language and library enhancements. But there are also numerous smaller changes throughout the library that are quite useful. I pored over all @since 1.8 notes in the API documentation and grouped the changes into categories for easy reference. In this chapter, you will find what is new for strings, numbers, math, collections, files, annotations, regular expressions, and JDBC.

The key points of this chapter are:

- Joining strings with a delimiter is finally easy: String.join(", ", a, b, c) instead of a + ", " + b + ", " + c.

- Integer types now support unsigned arithmetic.

- The Math class has methods to detect integer overflow.

- Use Math.floorMod(x, n) instead of x % n if x might be negative.

- There are new mutators in Collection (removeIf) and List (replaceAll, sort).

- Files.lines lazily reads a stream of lines.

- Files.list lazily lists the entries of a directory, and Files.walk traverses them recursively.

- There is finally official support for Base64 encoding.

- Annotations can now be repeated and applied to type uses.

- Convenient support for null parameter checks can be found in the Objects class.

8.1 Strings

A common task is to combine several strings, separating them with a delimiter such as ", " or "/". This has now been added to Java 8. The strings can come from an array or an Iterable<? extends CharSequence>:

```
String joined = String.join("/", "usr", "local", "bin"); // "usr/local/bin"
System.out.println(joined);
String ids = String.join(", ", ZoneId.getAvailableZoneIds());
System.out.println(ids);
   // All time zone identifiers, separated by commas
```

Think of join as the opposite of the String.split instance method. This is the only method added to the String class in Java 8.

 NOTE: As already mentioned in Chapter 2, the CharSequence interface provides a useful instance method codePoints that returns a stream of Unicode values, and a less useful method chars that returns a stream of UTF-16 code units.

8.2 Number Classes

Ever since Java 5, each of the seven numeric primitive type wrappers (i.e., not Boolean) had a static SIZE field that gives the size of the type in bits. You will be glad to know that there is now a BYTES field that reports the size in bytes, for those who cannot divide by eight.

All eight primitive type wrappers now have static hashCode methods that return the same hash code as the instance method, but without the need for boxing.

The five types Short, Integer, Long, Float, and Double now have static methods sum, max, and min, which can be useful as reduction functions in stream operations. The Boolean class has static methods logicalAnd, logicalOr, and logicalXor for the same purpose.

Integer types now support unsigned arithmetic. For example, instead of having a Byte represent the range from −128 to 127, you can call the static method Byte.toUnsignedInt(b) and get a value between 0 and 255. In general, with unsigned numbers, you lose the negative values and get twice the range of positive values. The Byte and Short classes have methods toUnsignedInt, and Byte, Short, and Integer have methods toUnsignedLong.

The Integer and Long classes have methods compareUnsigned, divideUnsigned, and remainderUnsigned to work with unsigned values. You don't need special methods for addition, subtraction, and multiplication. The + and - operators do the right thing already for unsigned values. Integer multiplication would overflow with unsigned integers larger than Integer.MAX_VALUE, so you should call toUnsignedLong and multiply them as long values.

NOTE: In order to work with unsigned numbers, you need to have a clear understanding of base-two arithmetic and the binary representation of negative numbers. In C and C++, mixing signed and unsigned types is a common cause of subtle errors. Java has wisely decided to stay away from this area, and has managed to live with only signed numbers for many years. The primary reason to use unsigned numbers is if you work with file formats or network protocols that require them.

The Float and Double classes have static methods isFinite. The call Double.isFinite(x) returns true if x is not infinity, negative infinity, or a NaN (not a number). In the past, you had to call the instance methods isInfinite and isNaN to get the same result.

Finally, the BigInteger class has instance methods (long | int | short | byte)ValueExact that return the value as a long, int, short, or byte, throwing an ArithmeticException if the value is not within the target range.

8.3 New Mathematical Functions

The Math class provides several methods for "exact" arithmetic that throw an exception when a result overflows. For example, 100000 * 100000 quietly gives the wrong result 1410065408, whereas multiplyExact(100000, 100000) throws an exception. The provided methods are (add | subtract | multiply | increment | decrement | negate)Exact, with int and long parameters. The toIntExact method converts a long to the equivalent int.

The floorMod and floorDiv methods aim to solve a long-standing problem with integer remainders. Consider the expression n % 2. Everyone knows that this is 0 if n is even and 1 if n is odd. Except, of course, when n is negative. Then it is –1. Why? When the first computers were built, someone had to make rules for how integer division and remainder should work for negative operands. Mathematicians had known the optimal (or "Euclidean") rule for a few hundred years: always leave the remainder ≥ 0. But, rather than open a math textbook, those pioneers came up with rules that seemed reasonable but are actually inconvenient.

Consider this problem. You compute the position of the hour hand of a clock. An adjustment is applied, and you want to normalize to a number between 0 and 11. That is easy: (position + adjustment) % 12. But what if adjustment is negative? Then you might get a negative number. So you have to introduce a branch, or use ((position + adjustment) % 12 + 12) % 12. Either way, it is a hassle.

The new floorMod method makes it easier: floorMod(position + adjustment, 12) always yields a value between 0 and 11.

 NOTE: Unfortunately, floorMod gives negative results for negative divisors, but that situation doesn't often occur in practice.

The nextDown method, defined for both double and float parameters, gives the next smaller floating-point number for a given number. For example, if you promise to produce a number < b, but you happen to have computed exactly b, then you can return Math.nextDown(b). (The corresponding Math.nextUp method exists since Java 6.)

 NOTE: All methods described in this section also exist in the StrictMath class.

8.4 Collections

The big change for the collections library is, of course, support for streams which you have seen in Chapter 2. There are some smaller changes as well.

8.4.1 Methods Added to Collection Classes

Table 8–1 shows miscellaneous methods added to collection classes and interfaces in Java 8, other than the stream, parallelStream, and spliterator methods.

You may wonder why the Stream interface has so many methods that accept lambda expressions but just one such method, removeIf, was added to the Collection interface. If you review the Stream methods, you will find that most of them return a single value or a stream of transformed values that are not present in the original stream. The exceptions are the filter and distinct methods. The removeIf method can be thought of as the opposite of filter, removing rather than producing all matches and carrying out the removal in place. The distinct method would be costly to provide on arbitrary collections.

The List interface has a replaceAll method, which is an in-place equivalent of map, and a sort method that is obviously useful.

Table 8–1 Methods Added to Collection Classes and Interface in Java 8

Class/Interface	New Methods
Iterable	forEach
Collection	removeIf
List	replaceAll, sort
Map	forEach, replace, replaceAll, remove(key, value) (removes only if key mapped to value), putIfAbsent, compute, computeIf(Absent | Present), merge
Iterator	forEachRemaining
BitSet	stream

The Map interface has a number of methods that are particularly important for maps accessed concurrently. See Chapter 6 for more information on these methods.

The Iterator interface has a forEachRemaining method that exhausts the iterator by feeding the remaining iterator elements to a function.

Finally, the BitSet class has a method that yields all members of the set as a stream of int values.

8.4.2 Comparators

The Comparator interface has a number of useful new methods, taking advantage of the fact that interfaces can now have concrete methods.

The static comparing method takes a "key extractor" function that maps a type T to a comparable type (such as String). The function is applied to the objects to be compared, and the comparison is then made on the returned keys. For example, suppose you have an array of Person objects. Here is how you can sort them by name:

```
Arrays.sort(people, Comparator.comparing(Person::getName));
```

You can chain comparators with the thenComparing method for breaking ties. For example,

```
Arrays.sort(people,
    Comparator.comparing(Person::getLastName)
    .thenComparing(Person::getFirstName));
```

If two people have the same last name, then the second comparator is used.

There are a few variations of these methods. You can specify a comparator to be used for the keys that the `comparing` and `thenComparing` methods extract. For example, here we sort people by the length of their names:

```
Arrays.sort(people, Comparator.comparing(Person::getName,
    (s, t) -> Integer.compare(s.length(), t.length()))));
```

Moreover, both the `comparing` and `thenComparing` methods have variants that avoid boxing of `int`, `long`, or `double` values. An easier way of producing the preceding operation would be

```
Arrays.sort(people, Comparator.comparingInt(p -> p.getName().length()));
```

If your key function can return `null`, you will like the `nullsFirst` and `nullsLast` adapters. These static methods take an existing comparator and modify it so that it doesn't throw an exception when encountering `null` values but ranks them as smaller or larger than regular values. For example, suppose `getMiddleName` returns a `null` when a person has no middle name. Then you can use `Comparator.comparing(Person::getMiddleName(), Comparator.nullsFirst(...))`.

The `nullsFirst` method needs a comparator—in this case, one that compares two strings. The `naturalOrder` method makes a comparator for any class implementing `Comparable`. A `Comparator.<String>naturalOrder()` is what we need. Here is the complete call for sorting by potentially null middle names. I use a static import of `java.util.Comparator.*`, to make the expression more legible. Note that the type for `naturalOrder` is inferred.

```
Arrays.sort(people, comparing(Person::getMiddleName,
    nullsFirst(naturalOrder()))));
```

The static `reverseOrder` method gives the reverse of the natural order. To reverse any comparator, use the `reversed` instance method. For example, `naturalOrder().reversed()` is the same as `reverseOrder()`.

8.4.3 The Collections Class

Java 6 introduced `NavigableSet` and `NavigableMap` interfaces that take advantage of the ordering of the elements or keys, providing efficient methods to locate, for any given value v, the smallest element ≥ or > v, or the largest element ≤ or < v. Now the `Collections` class supports these interfaces as it does other collections, with methods (unmodifiable | synchronized | checked | empty)Navigable(Set | Map).

A `checkedQueue` wrapper, that has apparently been overlooked all these years, has also been added. As a reminder, the `checked` wrappers have a `Class` parameter and throw a `ClassCastException` when you insert an element of the wrong type. These classes are intended as debugging aids. Suppose you declare a `Queue<Path>`, and somewhere in your code there is a `ClassCastException` trying to cast a `String` to a `Path`.

This could have happened because you passed the queue to a method void getMoreWork(Queue q) with no type parameter. Then, someone somewhere inserted a String into q. (Because the generic type was suppressed, the compiler could not detect that.) Much later, you took out that String, thinking it was a Path, and the error manifested itself. If you temporarily replace the queue with a CheckedQueue(new LinkedList<Path>, Path.class), then every insertion is checked at runtime, and you can locate the faulty insertion code.

Finally, there are emptySorted(Set|Map) methods that give lightweight instances of sorted collections, analogous to the empty(Set|Map) methods that have been around since Java 5.

8.5 Working with Files

Java 8 brings a small number of convenience methods that use streams for reading lines from files and for visiting directory entries. Also, there is finally an official way of performing Base64 encoding and decoding.

8.5.1 Streams of Lines

To read the lines of a file lazily, use the Files.lines method. It yields a stream of strings, one per line of input:

```
Stream<String> lines = Files.lines(path);
Optional<String> passwordEntry = lines.filter(s -> s.contains("password")).findFirst();
```

As soon as the first line containing password is found, no further lines are read from the underlying file.

 NOTE: Unlike the FileReader class, which was a portability nightmare since it opened files in the local character encoding, the Files.lines method defaults to UTF-8. You can specify other encodings by supplying a Charset argument.

You will want to close the underlying file. Fortunately, the Stream interface extends AutoCloseable. The streams that you have seen in Chapter 2 didn't need to close any resources. But the Files.lines method produces a stream whose close method closes the file. The easiest way to make sure the file is indeed closed is to use a Java 7 try-with-resources block:

```
try (Stream<String> lines = Files.lines(path)) {
   Optional<String> passwordEntry
      = lines.filter(s -> s.contains("password")).findFirst();
   ...
} // The stream, and hence the file, will be closed here
```

When a stream spawns another, the close methods are chained. Therefore, you can also write

```
try (Stream<String> filteredLines
    = Files.lines(path).filter(s -> s.contains("password"))) {
  Optional<String> passwordEntry = filteredLines.findFirst();
  ...
}
```

When filteredLines is closed, it closes the underlying stream, which closes the underlying file.

 NOTE: If you want to be notified when the stream is closed, you can attach an onClose handler. Here is how you can verify that closing filteredLines actually closes the underlying stream:

```
try (Stream<String> filteredLines
    = Files.lines(path).onClose(() -> System.out.println("Closing"))
        .filter(s -> s.contains("password"))) { ... }
```

If an IOException occurs as the stream fetches the lines, that exception is wrapped into an UncheckedIOException which is thrown out of the stream operation. (This subterfuge is necessary because stream operations are not declared to throw any checked exceptions.)

If you want to read lines from a source other than a file, use the BufferedReader.lines method instead:

```
try (BufferedReader reader
    = new BufferedReader(new InputStreamReader(url.openStream()))) {
  Stream<String> lines = reader.lines();
  ...
}
```

With this method, closing the resulting stream does *not* close the reader. For that reason, you must place the BufferedReader object, and not the stream object, into the header of the try statement.

 NOTE: Almost ten years ago, Java 5 introduced the Scanner class to replace the cumbersome BufferedReader. It is unfortunate that the Java 8 API designers decided to add the lines method to BufferedReader but not to Scanner.

8.5.2 Streams of Directory Entries

The static `Files.list` method returns a `Stream<Path>` that reads the entries of a directory. The directory is read lazily, making it possible to efficiently process directories with huge numbers of entries.

Since reading a directory involves a system resource that needs to be closed, you should use a try block:

```
try (Stream<Path> entries = Files.list(pathToDirectory)) {
    ...
}
```

 NOTE: Under the hood, the stream uses a `DirectoryStream`, a construct introduced in Java 7 for efficient traversal of huge directories. That interface has nothing to do with Java 8 streams; it extends `Iterable` so that it can be used in an enhanced for loop.

```
try (DirectoryStream stream = Files.newDirectoryStream(pathToDirectory)) {
    for (Path entry : stream) {
        ...
    }
}
```

In Java 8, just use `Files.list`.

The `list` method does not enter subdirectories. To process all descendants of a directory, use the `Files.walk` method instead.

```
try (Stream<Path> entries = Files.walk(pathToRoot)) {
    // Contains all descendants, visited in depth-first order
}
```

You can limit the depth of the tree that you want to visit by calling `Files.walk(pathToRoot, depth)`. Both `walk` methods have a varargs parameter of type `FileVisitOption...`, but there is currently only one option you can supply: `FOLLOW_LINKS` to follow symbolic links.

 NOTE: If you filter the paths returned by `walk` and your filter criterion involves the file attributes stored with a directory, such as size, creation time, or type (file, directory, symbolic link), then use the `find` method instead of `walk`. Call that method with a predicate function that accepts a path and a `BasicFileAttributes` object. The only advantage is efficiency. Since the directory is being read anyway, the attributes are readily available.

8.5.3 Base64 Encoding

The Base64 encoding encodes a sequence of bytes into a (longer) sequence of printable ASCII characters. It is used for binary data in email messages and "basic" HTTP authentication. For many years, the JDK had a nonpublic (and therefore unusable) class java.util.prefs.Base64 and an undocumented class sun.misc.BASE64Encoder. Finally, Java 8 provides a standard encoder and decoder.

The Base64 encoding uses 64 characters to encode six bits of information:

- 26 uppercase letters A . . . Z

- 26 lowercase letters a . . . z

- 10 digits 0 . . . 9

- 2 symbols, + and / (basic) or - and _ (URL- and filename-safe variant)

Normally, an encoded string has no line breaks, but the MIME standard used for email requires a "\r\n" line break every 76 characters.

For encoding, request a Base64.Encoder with one of the static methods getEncoder, getUrlEncoder, or getMimeEncoder of the Base64 class.

That class has methods to encode an array of bytes or a NIO ByteBuffer. For example,

```
Base64.Encoder encoder = Base64.getEncoder();
String original = username + ":" + password;
String encoded = encoder.encodeToString(original.getBytes(StandardCharsets.UTF_8));
```

Alternatively, you can "wrap" an output stream, so that all data sent to it is automatically encoded.

```
Path originalPath = ..., encodedPath = ...;
Base64.Encoder encoder = Base64.getMimeEncoder();
try (OutputStream output = Files.newOutputStream(encodedPath)) {
    Files.copy(originalPath, encoder.wrap(output));
}
```

To decode, reverse these operations:

```
Path encodedPath = ..., decodedPath = ...;
Base64.Decoder decoder = Base64.getMimeDecoder();
try (InputStream input = Files.newInputStream(encodedPath)) {
    Files.copy(decoder.wrap(input), decodedPath);
}
```

8.6 Annotations

Annotations are tags inserted into the source code that some tools can process. In Java SE, annotations are used for simple purposes, such as marking deprecated features or suppressing warnings. Annotations have a much more important role in Java EE where they are used to configure just about any aspect of an application, replacing painful boilerplate code and XML customization that was the bane of older Java EE versions.

Java 8 has two enhancements to annotation processing: repeated annotations and type use annotations. Moreover, reflection has been enhanced to report method parameter names. This has the potential to simplify annotations on method parameters.

8.6.1 Repeated Annotations

When annotations were first created, they were envisioned to mark methods and fields for processing, for example,

```
@PostConstruct public void fetchData() { ... } // Call after construction
@Resource("jdbc:derby:sample") private Connection conn;
    // Inject resource here
```

In this context, it made no sense to apply the same annotation twice. You can't inject a field in two ways. Of course, different annotations on the same element are fine and quite common:

```
@Stateless @Path("/service") public class Service { ... }
```

Soon, more and more uses for annotations emerged, leading to situations where one would have liked to repeat the same annotation. For example, to denote a composite key in a database, you need to specify multiple columns:

```
@Entity
@PrimaryKeyJoinColumn(name="ID")
@PrimaryKeyJoinColumn(name="REGION")
public class Item { ... }
```

Since that wasn't possible, the annotations were packed into a container annotation, like this:

```
@Entity
@PrimaryKeyJoinColumns({
    @PrimaryKeyJoinColumn(name="ID"),
    @PrimaryKeyJoinColumn(name="REGION")
})
public class Item { ... }
```

That's pretty ugly, and it is no longer necessary in Java 8.

As an annotation user, that is all you need to know. If your framework provider has enabled repeated annotations, you can just use them.

For a framework implementor, the story is not quite as simple. After all, the AnnotatedElement interface has a method

```
public <T extends Annotation> T getAnnotation(Class<T> annotationClass)
```

that gets *the* annotation of type T, if present. What should that method do if multiple annotations of the same type are present? Return the first one only? That could have all sorts of undesirable behavior with legacy code.

To solve this problem, the inventor of a repeatable annotation must

1. Annotate the annotation as @Repeatable

2. Provide a container annotation

For example, for a simple unit testing framework, we might define a repeatable @TestCase annotation, to be used like this:

```
@TestCase(params="4", expected="24")
@TestCase(params="0", expected="1")
public static long factorial(int n) { ... }
```

Here is how the annotation can be defined:

```
@Repeatable(TestCases.class)
@interface TestCase {
    String params();
    String expected();
}

@interface TestCases {
    TestCase[] value();
}
```

Whenever the user supplies two or more @TestCase annotations, they are automatically wrapped into a @TestCases annotation.

When annotation processing code calls element.getAnnotation(TestCase.class) on the element representing the factorial method, null is returned. This is because the element is actually annotated with the container annotation TestCases.

When implementing an annotation processor for your repeatable annotation, you will find it simpler to use the getAnnotationsByType method. The call element.getAnnotationsByType(TestCase.class) "looks through" any TestCases container and gives you an array of TestCase annotations.

NOTE: What I just described relates to processing runtime annotations with the reflection API. If you process source-level annotations, you use the `javax.lang.model` and `javax.annotation.processing` APIs. In those APIs, there is no support for "looking through" a container. You will need to process both the individual annotation (if it is supplied once) and the container (if the same annotation is supplied more than once).

8.6.2 Type Use Annotations

Prior to Java 8, an annotation was applied to a *declaration*. A declaration is a part of code that introduces a new name. Here are a couple of examples, with the declared name in bold:

```
@Entity public class Person { ... }
@SuppressWarnings("unchecked") List<Person> people = query.getResultList();
```

In Java 8, you can annotate any *type use*. This can be useful in combination with tools that check for common programming errors. One common error is throwing a `NullPointerException` because the programmer didn't anticipate that a reference might be null. Now suppose you annotated variables that you never want to be null as `@NonNull`. A tool can check that the following is correct:

```
private @NonNull List<String> names = new ArrayList<>();
...
names.add("Fred"); // No possibility of a NullPointerException
```

Of course, the tool should detect any statement that might cause names to become null:

```
names = null; // Null checker flags this as an error
names = readNames(); // OK if readNames returns a @NonNull String
```

It sounds tedious to put such annotations everywhere, but in practice, some of the drudgery can be avoided by simple heuristics. The null checker in the Checker Framework (http://types.cs.washington.edu/checker-framework) assumes that any nonlocal variables are implicitly `@NonNull`, but that local variables might be null unless the code shows otherwise. If a method may return a null, it needs to be annotated as `@Nullable`. That may not be any worse than documenting the nullness behavior. (The Java API documentation has over 5,000 occurrences of "NullPointerException.")

In the preceding example, the names variable was declared as `@NonNull`. That annotation was possible before Java 8. But how can one express that the list *elements* should be non-null? Logically, that would be

```
private List<@NonNull String> names;
```

It is this kind of annotation that was not possible before Java 8 but has now become legal.

 NOTE: These annotations are *not* part of standard Java. There are currently no standard annotations that are meaningful for type use. All examples in this section come from the Checker Framework or from the author's imagination.

Type use annotations can appear in the following places:

- With generic type arguments: `List<@NonNull String>`, `Comparator.<@NonNull String> reverseOrder()`.
- In any position of an array: `@NonNull String[][] words` (`words[i][j]` is not `null`), `String @NonNull [][] words` (`words` is not `null`), `String[] @NonNull [] words` (`words[i]` is not `null`).
- With superclasses and implemented interfaces: `class Image implements @Rectangular Shape`.
- With constructor invocations: `new @Path String("/usr/bin")`.
- With casts and instanceof checks: `(@Path String) input`, `if (input instanceof @Path String)`. (The annotations are only for use by external tools. They have no effect on the behavior of a cast or an `instanceof` check.)
- With exception specifications: `public Person read() throws @Localized IOException`.
- With wildcards and type bounds: `List<@ReadOnly ? extends Person>`, `List<? extends @ReadOnly> Person`.
- With method and constructor references: `@Immutable Person::getName`.

There are a few type positions that cannot be annotated:

```
@NonNull String.class // Illegal—cannot annotate class literal
import java.lang.@NonNull String; // Illegal—cannot annotate import
```

It is also impossible to annotate an annotation. For example, given `@NonNull String name`, you cannot annotate `@NonNull`. (You can supply a separate annotation, but it would apply to the `name` declaration.)

The practical use of these annotations hinges on the viability of the tools. If you are interested in exploring the potential of extended type checking, a good place to start is the Checker Framework tutorial at http://types.cs.washington.edu/checker-framework/tutorial.

8.6.3 Method Parameter Reflection

The names of parameters are now available through reflection. That is promising because it can reduce annotation boilerplate. Consider a typical JAX-RS method

```
Person getEmployee(@PathParam("dept") Long dept, @QueryParam("id") Long id)
```

In almost all cases, the parameter names are the same as the annotation arguments, or they can be made to be the same. If the annotation processor could read the parameter names, then one could simply write

```
Person getEmployee(@PathParam Long dept, @QueryParam Long id)
```

This is possible in Java 8, with the new class java.lang.reflect.Parameter.

Unfortunately, for the necessary information to appear in the classfile, the source must be compiled as javac -parameters SourceFile.java. Let's hope annotation writers will enthusiastically embrace this mechanism, so there will be momentum to drop that compiler flag in the future.

8.7 Miscellaneous Minor Changes

We end this chapter with miscellaneous minor changes that you might find useful. This section covers the new features of the Objects, Logger, and Locale classes, as well as changes to regular expressions and JDBC.

8.7.1 Null Checks

The Objects class has static predicate methods isNull and nonNull that can be useful for streams. For example,

```
stream.anyMatch(Objects::isNull)
```

checks whether a stream contains a null, and

```
stream.filter(Objects::nonNull)
```

gets rid of all of them.

8.7.2 Lazy Messages

The log, logp, severe, warning, info, config, fine, finer, and finest methods of the java.util.Logger class now support lazily constructed messages.

For example, consider the call

```
logger.finest("x: " + x + ", y:" + y);
```

The message string is formatted even when the logging level is such that it would never be used. Instead, use

```
logger.finest(() -> "x: " + x + ", y:" + y);
```

Now the lambda expression is only evaluated at the FINEST logging level, when the cost of the additional lambda invocation is presumably the least of one's problems.

The `requireNonNull` of the `Objects` class (which is described in Chapter 9) also has a version that computes the message string lazily.

```
this.directions = Objects.requireNonNull(directions,
    () -> "directions for " + this.goal + " must not be null");
```

In the common case that `directions` is not `null`, `this.directions` is simply set to `directions`. If `directions` is `null`, the lambda is invoked, and a `NullPointerException` is thrown whose message is the returned string.

8.7.3 Regular Expressions

Java 7 introduced named capturing groups. For example, a valid regular expression is

```
(?<city>[\p{L} ]+),\s*(?<state>[A-Z]{2})
```

In Java 8, you can use the names in the `start`, `end`, and `group` methods of `Matcher`:

```
Matcher matcher = pattern.matcher(input);
if (matcher.matches()) {
    String city = matcher.group("city");
    ...
}
```

The `Pattern` class has a `splitAsStream` method that splits a `CharSequence` along a regular expression:

```
String contents = new String(Files.readAllBytes(path), StandardCharsets.UTF_8);
Stream<String> words = Pattern.compile("[\\P{L}]+").splitAsStream(contents);
```

All nonletter sequences are word separators.

The method `asPredicate` can be used to filter strings that match a regular expression:

```
Stream<String> acronyms = words.filter(Pattern.compile("[A-Z]{2,}").asPredicate());
```

8.7.4 Locales

A locale specifies everything you need to know to present information to a user with local preferences concerning language, date formats, and so on. For example, an American user prefers to see a date formatted as December 24, 2013 or 12/24/2013, whereas a German user expects 24. Dezember 2013 or 24.12.2013.

It used to be that locales were simple, consisting of location, language, and (for a few oddball cases, such as the Norwegians who have two spelling systems) variants. But those oddball cases mushroomed, and the Internet Engineering Task Force issued its "Best Current Practices" memo BCP 47 (http://tools.ietf.org/html/bcp47) to bring some order into the chaos. Nowadays, a locale is composed of up to five components.

1. A language, specified by two or three lowercase letters, such as en (English) or de (German or, in German, Deutsch).

2. A script, specified by four letters with an initial uppercase, such as Latn (Latin), Cyrl (Cyrillic), or Hant (traditional Chinese characters). This is useful because some languages, such as Serbian, are written in Latin or Cyrillic, and some Chinese readers prefer the traditional over the simplified characters.

3. A country, specified by two uppercase letters or three digits, such as US (United States) or CH (Switzerland).

4. Optionally, a variant. Variants are not common any more. For example, the Nynorsk spelling of Norwegian is now expressed with a different language code, nn, instead of a variant NY of the language no.

5. Optionally, an extension. Extensions describe local preferences for calendars (such as the Japanese calendar), numbers (Thai digits), and so on. The Unicode standard specifies some of these extensions. Such extensions start with u- and a two-letter code specifying whether the extension deals with the calendar (ca), numbers (nu), and so on. For example, the extension u-nu-thai denotes the use of Thai numerals. Other extensions are entirely arbitrary and start with x-, such as x-java.

You can still construct a locale the old-fashioned way, such as new Locale("en", "US"), but since Java 7 you can simply call Locale.forLanguageTag("en-US"). Java 8 adds methods for finding locales that match user needs.

A *language range* is a string that denotes the locale characteristics that a user desires, with * for wildcards. For example, a German speaker in Switzerland might prefer anything in German, followed by anything in Switzerland. This is expressed with two Locale.LanguageRange objects specified with strings "de" and "*-CH". One can optionally specify a weight between 0 and 1 when constructing a Locale.LanguageRange.

Given a list of weighted language ranges and a collection of locales, the filter method produces a list of matching locales, in descending order of match quality:

```
List<Locale.LanguageRange> ranges = Stream.of("de", "*-CH")
    .map(Locale.LanguageRange::new)
    .collect(Collectors.toList());
    // A list containing the Locale.LanguageRange objects for the given strings
List<Locale> matches = Locale.filter(ranges,
    Arrays.asList(Locale.getAvailableLocales()));
    // The matching locales: de, de-CH, de-AT, de-LU, de-DE, de-GR, fr-CH, it_CH
```

The static lookup method just finds the best locale:

```
Locale bestMatch = Locale.lookup(ranges, locales);
```

In this case, the best match is de, which isn't very interesting. But if locales contains a more restricted set of locales, such as those in which a document was available, then this mechanism can be useful.

8.7.5 JDBC

In Java 8, JDBC has been updated to version 4.2. There are a few minor changes.

The Date, Time, and Timestamp classes in the java.sql package have methods to convert from and to their java.time analogs LocalDate, LocalTime, and LocalDateTime.

The Statement class has a method executeLargeUpdate for executing an update whose row count exceeds Integer.MAX_VALUE.

JDBC 4.1 (which was a part of Java 7) specified a generic method getObject(column, type) for Statement and ResultSet, where type is a Class instance. For example, URL url = result.getObject("link", URL.class) retrieves a DATALINK as a URL. Now the corresponding setObject method is provided as well.

Exercises

1. Write a program that adds, subtracts, divides, and compares numbers between 0 and $2^{32} - 1$, using int values and unsigned operations. Show why divideUnsigned and remainderUnsigned are necessary.

2. For which integer n does Math.negateExact(n) throw an exception? (Hint: There is only one.)

3. Euclid's algorithm (which is over two thousand years old) computes the greatest common divisor of two numbers as gcd(a, b) = a if b is zero, and gcd(b, rem(a, b)) otherwise, where rem is the remainder. Clearly, the gcd should not be negative, even if a or b are (since its negation would then be a greater divisor). Implement the algorithm with %, floorMod, and a rem function that produces the mathematical (non-negative) remainder. Which of the three gives you the least hassle with negative values?

4. The Math.nextDown(x) method returns the next smaller floating-point number than x, just in case some random process hit x exactly, and we promised a number < x. Can this really happen? Consider double r = 1 - generator. nextDouble(), where generator is an instance of java.util.Random. Can it ever yield 1? That is, can generator.nextDouble() ever yield 0? The documentation says it can yield any value between 0 inclusive and 1 exclusive. But, given that there are 2^{53} such floating-point numbers, will you ever get a zero? Indeed, you

do. The random number generator computes the next seed as next$(s) = s \cdot m + a \% N$, where $m = 25214903917$, $a = 11$, and $N = 2^{48}$. The inverse of m modulo N is $v = 246154705703781$, and therefore you can compute the predecessor of a seed as prev$(s) = (s - a) \cdot v \% N$. To make a `double`, two random numbers are generated, and the top 26 and 27 bits are taken each time. When s is 0, next(s) is 11, so that's what we want to hit: two consecutive numbers whose top bits are zero. Now, working backwards, let's start with $s = $ prev(prev(prev(0))). Since the `Random` constructor sets $s = (initialSeed$ ^ $m) \% N$, offer it $s = $ prev(prev(prev(0))) ^ $m = 164311266871034$, and you'll get a zero after two calls to `nextDouble`. But that is still too obvious. Generate a million predecessors, using a stream of course, and pick the minimum seed. Hint: You will get a zero after 376050 calls to `nextDouble`.

5. At the beginning of Chapter 2, we counted long words in a list as `words.stream().filter(w -> w.length() > 12).count()`. Do the same with a lambda expression, but without using streams. Which operation is faster for a long list?

6. Using only methods of the `Comparator` class, define a comparator for `Point2D` which is a total ordering (that is, the comparator only returns zero for equal objects). Hint: First compare the x-coordinates, then the y-coordinates. Do the same for `Rectangle2D`.

7. Express `nullsFirst(naturalOrder()).reversed()` without calling `reversed`.

8. Write a program that demonstrates the benefits of the `CheckedQueue` class.

9. Write methods that turn a `Scanner` into a stream of words, lines, integers, or `double` values. Hint: Look at the source code for `BufferedReader.lines`.

10. Unzip the `src.zip` file from the JDK. Using `Files.walk`, find all Java files that contain the keywords `transient` and `volatile`.

11. Write a program that gets the contents of a password-protected web page. Call `URLConnection connection = url.openConnection();`. Form the string *username: password* and encode it in Base64. Then call `connection.setRequestProperty( "Authorization", "Basic " + encoded string)`, followed by `connection.connect()` and `connection.getInputStream()`.

12. Implement the `TestCase` annotation and a program that loads a class with such annotations and invokes the annotated methods, checking whether they yield the expected values. Assume that parameters and return values are integers.

13. Repeat the preceding exercise, but build a source-level annotation processor emitting a program that, when executed, runs the tests in its `main` method. (See Horstmann and Cornell, *Core Java, 9th Edition, Volume 2*, Section 10.6 for an introduction into processing source-level annotations.)

14. Demonstrate the use of the `Objects.requireNonNull` method and show how it leads to more useful error messages.

15. Using `Files.lines` and `Pattern.asPredicate`, write a program that acts like the `grep` utility, printing all lines that contain a match for a regular expression.

16. Use a regular expression with named capturing groups to parse a line containing a city, state, and zip code. Accept both 5- and 9-digit zip codes.

Java 7 Features That You May Have Missed

Chapter 9

When Java 7 was released, most reviewers focused on the new language features: strings in switch statements, binary literals, underscores in literals, improved type inference, and so on. In this chapter, I will write about some of the library changes that haven't been discussed so much and that I have found far more useful in daily work than switching on strings or binary literals. I cover one language change that is very useful in daily work—the try-with-resources statement.

The key points of this chapter are:

- Use the try-with-resources statement with any object that implements `AutoCloseable`.

- The try-with-resources statement rethrows the primary exception if closing a resource throws another exception.

- You can catch unrelated exceptions with a single catch clause.

- The exceptions for reflective operations now have a common superclass `ReflectiveOperationException`.

- Use the `Path` interface instead of the `File` class.

- You can read and write all characters, or all lines, of a text file with a single command.

- The `Files` class has static methods for copying, moving, and deleting files, and for creating files and directories.

- Use `Objects.equals` for null-safe equality testing.

- `Objects.hash` makes it simple to implement the `hashCode` method.
- When comparing numbers in a comparator, use the static `compare` method.
- Applets and Java Web Start applications continue to be supported in corporate environments, but they may no longer be viable for home users.
- Everyone's favorite trivial change: "+1" can now be converted to an integer without throwing an exception.
- Changes in `ProcessBuilder` make it simple to redirect standard input, output, and error streams.

9.1 Exception Handling Changes

I start this chapter with the Java 7 features for exception handling, since they have a major impact on writing reliable programs. I briefly review the try-with-resources statement before moving on to more subtle changes.

9.1.1 The try-with-resources Statement

Java 7 provides a useful shortcut to the code pattern

```
open a resource
try {
    work with the resource
}
finally {
    close the resource
}
```

provided the resource belongs to a class that implements the `AutoCloseable` interface. That interface has a single method

```
void close() throws Exception
```

> NOTE: There is also a `Closeable` interface. It is a subinterface of `AutoCloseable`, also with a single `close` method, but that method is declared to throw an `IOException`.

In its simplest variant, the try-with-resources statement has the form

```
try (Resource res = ...) {
    work with res
}
```

When the try block exits, res.close() is called automatically. Here is a typical example—reading all words of a file:

```
try (Scanner in = new Scanner(Paths.get("/usr/share/dict/words"))) {
   while (in.hasNext())
      System.out.println(in.next().toLowerCase());
}
```

When the block exits normally, or when there is an exception, the in.close() method is called, exactly as if you had used a finally block.

You can specify multiple resources, for example:

```
try (Scanner in = new Scanner(Paths.get("/usr/share/dict/words"));
     PrintWriter out = new PrintWriter("/tmp/out.txt")) {
   while (in.hasNext())
      out.println(in.next().toLowerCase());
}
```

No matter how the block exits, both in and out are closed if they were constructed. This was surprisingly difficult to implement correctly prior to Java 7 (see Exercise 1).

 NOTE: A try-with-resources statement can itself have catch clauses and a finally clause. These are executed after closing the resources. In practice, it's probably not a good idea to pile so much onto a single try statement.

9.1.2 Suppressed Exceptions

Whenever you work with input or output, there is an awkward problem with closing the resource after an exception. Suppose an IOException occurs and then, when closing the resource, the call to close throws another exception.

Which exception will actually be caught? In Java, an exception thrown in a finally clause discards the previous exception. This sounds inconvenient, and it is. After all, the user is likely to be much more interested in the original exception.

The try-with-resources statement reverses this behavior. When an exception is thrown in a close method of one of the AutoCloseable objects, the original exception gets rethrown, and the exceptions from calling close are caught and attached as "suppressed" exceptions. This is a very useful mechanism that would be tedious to implement by hand (see Exercise 2).

When you catch the primary exception, you can retrieve those secondary exceptions by calling the getSuppressed method:

```
try {
    ...
} catch (IOException ex) {
    Throwable[] secondaryExceptions = ex.getSuppressed();
}
```

If you want to implement such a mechanism yourself in the (hopefully rare) situation when you can't use the try-with-resources statement, call

```
ex.addSuppressed(secondaryException);
```

NOTE: The classes Throwable, Exception, RuntimeException, and Error have constructors with an option for disabling suppressed exceptions and for disabling stack traces. When suppressed exceptions are disabled, calling addSuppressed has no effect, and getSuppressed returns a zero-length array. When stack traces are disabled, calls to fillInStackTrace have no effect, and getStackTrace returns a zero-length array. This can be useful for VM errors when memory is low, or for programming languages on the VM that use exceptions to break out of nested method calls.

CAUTION: Detecting secondary exceptions only works when it isn't actively sabotaged. In particular, if you use a Scanner, and if input fails, and then closing fails, the Scanner class catches the input exception, closes the resource and catches that exception, and then throws an entirely different exception, without linking the suppressed exceptions.

9.1.3 Catching Multiple Exceptions

As of Java SE 7, you can catch multiple exception types in the same catch clause. For example, suppose that the action for missing files and unknown hosts is the same. Then you can combine the catch clauses:

```
try {
    Code that might throw exceptions
}
catch (FileNotFoundException | UnknownHostException ex) {
    Emergency action for missing files and unknown hosts
}
catch (IOException ex) {
    Emergency action for all other I/O problems
}
```

This feature is only needed when catching exception types that are not subclasses of one another.

Catching multiple exceptions doesn't just make your code look simpler but is also more efficient. The generated bytecodes contain a single block for the shared catch clause.

 NOTE: When you catch multiple exceptions, the exception variable is implicitly final. For example, you cannot assign a new value to ex in the body of the clause catch (`FileNotFoundException | UnknownHostException ex`) { ... }.

9.1.4 Easier Exception Handling for Reflective Methods

In the past, when you called a reflective method, you had to catch multiple unrelated checked exceptions. For example, suppose you construct a class and invoke its main method:

```
Class.forName(className).getMethod("main").invoke(null, new String[] {});
```

This statement can cause a `ClassNotFoundException`, `NoSuchMethodException`, `IllegalAccessException`, or `InvocationTargetException`.

Of course, you can use the feature described in the preceding section and combine them in a single clause:

```
catch (ClassNotFoundException | NoSuchMethodException
    | IllegalAccessException | InvocationTargetException ex) { ... }
```

However, that is still very tedious. Plainly, it is bad design not to provide a common superclass for related exceptions. That design flaw has been remedied in Java 7. A new superclass `ReflectiveOperationException` has been introduced so that you can catch all of these exceptions in a single handler:

```
catch (ReflectiveOperationException ex) { ... }
```

9.2 Working with Files

The try-with-resources statement is my favorite feature in Java 7, but the file handling improvements are a close second. Operations that used to be tedious, such as reading a file into a string, or copying a file to another, are now as easy as they should have been all along. These are part of the "NIO2" effort, which refreshes the NIO ("new I/O") library introduced in 2002 with Java 1.4. (It is never a good idea to include "new" in a product name—what is new today will invariably become old, and the name will look silly.)

Before you can learn how to carry out these easy file operations, you have to learn about the Path interface that replaces the File class. Next, you will see how to read and write files. Finally, we will turn to file and directory operations.

9.2.1 Paths

A `Path` is a sequence of directory names, optionally followed by a file name. The first component of a path may be a root component, such as / or C:\. The permissible root components depend on the file system. A path that starts with a root component is *absolute*. Otherwise, it is *relative*. For example, here we construct an absolute and a relative path. For the absolute path, we assume a computer running a Unix-like file system.

```
Path absolute = Paths.get("/", "home", "cay");
Path relative = Paths.get("myprog", "conf", "user.properties");
```

The static `Paths.get` method receives one or more strings, which it joins with the path separator of the default file system (/ for a Unix-like file system, \ for Windows). It then parses the result, throwing an `InvalidPathException` if the result is not a valid path in the given file system. The result is a `Path` object.

You can also provide a string with separators to the `Paths.get` method:

```
Path homeDirectory = Paths.get("/home/cay");
```

 NOTE: Just like a `File` object, a `Path` object does not have to correspond to a file that actually exists. It is merely an abstract sequence of names. To create a file, first make a path, then call a method to create the corresponding file.

It is very common to combine or resolve paths. The call `p.resolve(q)` returns a path according to these rules:

* If q is absolute, then the result is q.

* Otherwise, the result is "p then q," according to the rules of the file system.

For example, suppose your application needs to find its configuration file relative to the home directory. Here is how you can combine the paths:

```
Path configPath = homeDirectory.resolve("myprog/conf/user.properties");
    // Same as homeDirectory.resolve(Paths.get("myprog/conf/user.properties"));
```

There is a convenience method `resolveSibling` that resolves against a path's parent, yielding a sibling path. For example, if `workPath` is /home/cay/myprog/work, the call

```
Path tempPath = workPath.resolveSibling("temp");
```

yields /home/cay/myprog/temp.

The opposite of `resolve` is `relativize`. The call `p.relativize(r)` yields the path q which, when resolved with p, yields r. For example,

```
Paths.get("/home/cay").relativize(Paths.get("/home/fred/myprog"))
```

yields ../fred/myprog, assuming we have a file system that uses .. to denote the parent directory.

The normalize method removes any redundant . and .. components (or whatever the file system may deem redundant). For example, normalizing the path /home/cay/../fred/./myprog yields /home/fred/myprog.

The toAbsolutePath method yields the absolute path of a given path. If the path is not already absolute, it is resolved against the "user directory"—that is, the directory from which the JVM was invoked. For example, if you launched a program from /home/cay/myprog, then Paths.get("config").toAbsolutePath() returns /home/cay/myprog/config.

The Path interface has many useful methods for taking paths apart and combining them with other paths. This code sample shows some of the most useful ones:

```
Path p = Paths.get("/home", "cay", "myprog.properties");
Path parent = p.getParent(); // The path /home/cay
Path file = p.getFileName(); // The last element, myprog.properties
Path root = p.getRoot(); // The initial segment / (null for a relative path)
```

 NOTE: Occasionally, you may need to interoperate with legacy APIs that use the File class instead of the Path interface. The Path interface has a toFile method, and the File class has a toPath method.

9.2.2 Reading and Writing Files

The Files class makes quick work of common file operations. For example, you can easily read the entire contents of a file:

```
byte[] bytes = Files.readAllBytes(path);
```

If you want to read the file as a string, call readAllBytes followed by

```
String content = new String(bytes, StandardCharsets.UTF_8);
```

But if you want the file as a sequence of lines, call

```
List<String> lines = Files.readAllLines(path);
```

Conversely, if you want to write a string, call

```
Files.write(path, content.getBytes(StandardCharsets.UTF_8));
```

You can also write a collection of lines with

```
Files.write(path, lines);
```

To append to a given file, use

```
Files.write(path, lines, StandardOpenOption.APPEND);
```

NOTE: By default, all methods of the `Files` class that read or write characters use the UTF-8 encoding. In the (hopefully unlikely) case that you need a different encoding, you can supply a `Charset` argument. Contrast with the `String` constructor and `getBytes` method which use the platform default. Commonly used desktop operating systems still use archaic 8-bit encodings that are incompatibe with UTF-8, so we must specify the encoding whenever converting between strings and bytes.

When you work with text files of moderate length, it is usually simplest to process the contents as a single string or list of strings. If your files are large or binary, you can still use the familiar streams or readers/writers:

```
InputStream in = Files.newInputStream(path);
OutputStream out = Files.newOutputStream(path);
Reader reader = Files.newBufferedReader(path);
Writer writer = Files.newBufferedWriter(path);
```

These convenience methods save you from having to deal with `FileInputStream`, `FileOutputStream`, `BufferedReader`, or `BufferedWriter`.

Occasionally, you may have an `InputStream` (for example, from a URL) and you want to save its contents to a file. Use

```
Files.copy(in, path);
```

Conversely,

```
Files.copy(path, out);
```

copies a file to an output stream.

9.2.3 Creating Files and Directories

To create a new directory, call

```
Files.createDirectory(path);
```

All but the last component in the path must already exist. To create intermediate directories as well, use

```
Files.createDirectories(path);
```

You can create an empty file with

```
Files.createFile(path);
```

The call throws an exception if the file already exists. The check for existence and the creation are atomic. If the file doesn't exist, it is created before anyone else has a chance to do the same.

The call Files.exists(path) method checks whether the given file or directory exists, but of course it might cease to exist by the time the method has returned.

There are convenience methods for creating a temporary file or directory in a given or system-specific location.

```
Path newPath = Files.createTempFile(dir, prefix, suffix);
Path newPath = Files.createTempFile(prefix, suffix);
Path newPath = Files.createTempDirectory(dir, prefix);
Path newPath = Files.createTempDirectory(prefix);
```

Here, dir is a Path, and prefix/suffix are strings which may be null. For example, the call Files.createTempFile(null, ".txt") might return a path such as /tmp/1234405522364837194.txt.

 NOTE: To read files from a directory, use the Files.list and Files.walk methods described in Chapter 8.

9.2.4 Copying, Moving, and Deleting Files

To copy a file from one location to another, simply call

```
Files.copy(fromPath, toPath);
```

To move a file (that is, copy and delete the original), call

```
Files.move(fromPath, toPath);
```

You can also use this command to move an empty directory.

The copy or move will fail if the target exists. If you want to overwrite an existing target, use the REPLACE_EXISTING option. If you want to copy all file attributes, use the COPY_ATTRIBUTES option. You can supply both like this:

```
Files.copy(fromPath, toPath, StandardCopyOption.REPLACE_EXISTING,
    StandardCopyOption.COPY_ATTRIBUTES);
```

You can specify that a move should be atomic. Then you are assured that either the move completed successfully, or the source continues to be present. Use the ATOMIC_MOVE option:

```
Files.move(fromPath, toPath, StandardCopyOption.ATOMIC_MOVE);
```

Finally, to delete a file, simply call

```
Files.delete(path);
```

This method throws an exception if the file doesn't exist, so instead you may want to use

```
boolean deleted = Files.deleteIfExists(path);
```

The deletion methods can also be used to remove an empty directory.

 NOTE: There is no convenient method for removing or copying a nonempty directory. See the API documentation of the `FileVisitor` interface for code outlines that achieve these tasks.

9.3 Implementing the `equals`, `hashCode`, and `compareTo` Methods

Java 7 introduces several methods that make it more convenient to deal with null values in the ubiquitous `equals` and `hashCode`, and with numeric comparisons in `compareTo`.

9.3.1 Null-safe Equality Testing

Suppose you have to implement the `equals` method for this class:

```
public class Person {
    private String first;
    private String last;
    ...
}
```

First, there is the drudgery of casting the parameter to a `Person`:

```
public boolean equals(Object otherObject) {
    if (this == otherObject) return true;
    if (otherObject == null) return false;
    if (getClass() != otherObject.getClass()) return false;
    Person other = (Person) otherObject;
    ...
}
```

Unfortunately, that drudgery isn't simplified yet. But now it gets better. Instead of worrying that `first` or `last` might be `null`, just call

```
return Objects.equals(first, other.first) && Objects.equals(last, other.last);
```

The call `Objects.equals(a, b)` returns `true` if both a and b are `null`, `false` if only a is `null`, and `a.equals(b)` otherwise.

 NOTE: In general, it is a good idea to call `Objects.equals(a, b)` when you would have called `a.equals(b)` before.

9.3.2 Computing Hash Codes

Consider computing a hash code for the preceding class. The `Objects.hashCode` method returns a code of 0 for a `null` argument, so you can implement the body of your `hashCode` method like this:

```
return 31 * Objects.hashCode(first) + Objects.hashCode(last);
```

But it gets better than that. The varargs method `Objects.hash`, introduced in Java 7, lets you specify any sequence of values, and their hash codes get combined:

```
return Objects.hash(first, last);
```

 NOTE: `Objects.hash` simply calls `Arrays.hash`, which existed since Java 5. But it isn't a varargs method, making it less convenient.

 NOTE: There has always been a null-safe way of calling `toString` as `String.valueOf(obj)`. If `obj` is `null`, the string `"null"` is returned. If you don't like that, you can use `Objects.toString` and supply the value to be used for `null`, for example `Objects.toString(obj, "")`.

9.3.3 Comparing Numeric Types

When you compare integers in a comparator, it is tempting to return the difference between them since you are allowed to return any negative or positive number—only the sign matters. For example, suppose you are implementing a Point class:

```
public int compareTo(Point other) {
    int diff = x - other.x; // Risk of overflow
    if (diff != 0) return diff;
    return y - other.y;
}
```

But that is problematic. If x is large and `other.x` is negative, the difference can overflow. That makes `compareTo` rather tedious (see Exercise 8).

As of Java 7, use the static `Integer.compare` method:

```
public int compareTo(Point other) {
    int diff = Integer.compare(x, other.x); // No risk of overflow
    if (diff != 0) return diff;
    return Integer.compare(y, other.y);
}
```

In the past, some people used `new Integer(x).compareTo(other.x)`, but that creates two boxed integers. The static method has `int` parameters.

The static `compare` method has also been added to `Long`, `Short`, `Byte`, and `Boolean`. If you need to compare two `char` values, you can safely subtract them because the result will not overflow. (The same is true for `short` or `byte`, of course.)

 NOTE: The static `compare` method existed for `Double` and `Float` since Java 1.2.

9.4 Security Requirements

When Java 1.0 was introduced in 1995 to an astounded world, the feature that caught everyone's imagination were applets: remotely served code that runs inside the user's web browser. The designers of Java knew perfectly well that executing remote code is a security risk, so they designed a "sandbox" model that stopped any damaging instructions in their tracks.

Soon thereafter, academic researchers found some implementation flaws that were promptly fixed, and other academic researchers groused in general over the fact that the Java security model was rather complex and there was little assurance that its darker corners are safe from assault. At the time, I didn't take that very seriously because the vast majority of Java applet consumers used Microsoft Windows, which was far less secure and far more complex.

Applets were limited to visual effects and network connections to the originating host, which many application writers found limiting. They wanted local device access for storage, printing, and so on. In 2001, Java Web Start delivered an extension of the sandbox that was quite powerful, comparable to today's HTML 5 extensions for local device access. Unfortunately, Java Web Start was poorly understood, not integrated with applets, and not maintained with any vigor.

Instead, many application developers simply signed their web-delivered programs, which gave them full permission to do anything on the user's machine. Signing certificates from commercial entities are within reach of anyone willing to endure some cost and pain. It was also possible to apply a meaningless self-signed certificate, or have users agree to run an applet without a certificate. Warnings were toned down from one release to the next until they became background noise. This was very bad.

Meanwhile, Microsoft, with an enormous engineering effort, got better at closing Windows loopholes, and it became worthwhile for hackers to look at obscure Java vulnerabilities instead. When Oracle purchased Sun in 2010, they inherited a very limited infrastructure for dealing with such attacks and no reliable means of updating client virtual machines. Hackers became increasingly successful in exploiting Java implementation bugs. In this regard, the early researchers who warned of a large attack surface in the Java security model were entirely justified. It took Oracle until 2013 to credibly respond to attacks. Management of client VMs is still a work in progress.

As of today, Oracle signals that it is no longer focused on securing home users' Java applets and Web Start applications (collectively called rich internet applications, or RIAs). Oracle continues to close Java vulnerabilities, and develops tools that are suitable for corporate deployment, so that legacy RIAs can be deployed safely. From a commercial standpoint, this makes sense. Home users are expected to migrate away from PCs to tablets and smartphones. These devices don't support a Java VM in the browser. And business users are a plausible revenue target for maintaining legacy applications.

With successive Java 7 releases, Oracle has tightened the security rules. As of January 2014, RIAs running outside the sandbox need to be signed by a commercial certificate authority. Another requirement is designed to thwart "repurposing attacks." Currently, it is possible to grab a legitimately signed JAR file from a third party and serve it from a hacker site, exploiting some vulnerability in that third-party app. As of January 2014, all JARs *must* have a manifest entry

```
Permissions: sandbox
```

or

```
Permissions: all-permissions
```

Since the manifest entry is inside the JAR file, it is signed and cannot be modified afterwards. The Java client will not permit sandbox execution of an all-permission client, which prevents "drive-by" attacks where an applet runs without any user consent. Of course, it is still possible to attack users who are habituated to agree to any security dialogs. To make that harder, another, as yet optional, manifest entry has been added:

```
Codebase: https://www.mycompany.com www.mycompany.com:8080
```

only allows the application to be loaded from one of the given URLs.

 NOTE: It has always been possible to call applets from JavaScript—another dubious decision from the point of view of the security minded. If you are using that feature in your application, you can minimize the repurposing risk by adding an entry `Caller-Allowable-Codebase: https://www.mycompany.com` to the manifest before signing.

Overall, these developments are very sad. Java held great promise as a universal execution platform for remote code. If Java had offered a more compelling sandbox, if nonsandbox code had been more aggressively controlled, if there had been consistent response to security breaches, and if client VMs had been reliably updated, Java might still be that universal platform. But there is no use dwelling on what might have been. At this point, Java is no longer a viable platform for widespread distribution of client applications over the Internet.

If you maintain an applet or Java Web Start application for home users, the message is clear: Move away from it. If your application serves a specialized audience (for example, software development, image editing, or document processing), make your users install Java or bundle a JVM with your installer. If you target a general audience—such as game players—consider using another technology, perhaps HTML 5.

 NOTE: If you decide to make your users install Java, you face another hurdle. If you direct Windows users to the installer at http://java.com, they will receive the widely reviled toolbar for Ask.com by default (see Figure 9–1). You have a couple of alternatives. You could have your users install the JDK, directing them to www.oracle.com/technetwork/java/javase/downloads and providing them with instructions for traversing that ever-changing page. Or you could bundle a JVM, which you are then obligated to update since no effective update mechanism is supplied by Oracle.

Figure 9–1   By default, the Windows JRE installer installs the Ask toolbar.

In a corporate environment, you can effectively secure Java RIAs, provided you have control over the applications and the client machines. You will need to tightly manage the application packaging and be ready to update client VMs when security updates become available.

 NOTE: To more tightly manage corporate RIAs, you can provide *deployment rulesets* on end-user machines. The process—not for the faint of heart—is explained at http://docs.oracle.com/javase/7/docs/technotes/guides/jweb/deployment_rules.html.

9.5 Miscellaneous Changes

As in the preceding chapter, this section describes a number of smaller features that you may find interesting or useful.

9.5.1 Converting Strings to Numbers

Prior to JDK 1.7, what was the result of the following code segment?

```
double x = Double.parseDouble("+1.0");
int n = Integer.parseInt("+1");
```

Pat yourself on the back if you knew the answer: +1.0 has always been a valid floating-point number, but until Java 7, +1 was not a valid integer.

This has now been fixed for all the various methods that construct int, long, short, byte, and BigInteger values from strings. There are more of them than you may think. In addition to parse(Int | Long | Short | Byte), there are decode methods that work with hexadecimal and octal inputs, and valueOf methods that yield wrapper objects. The BigInteger(String) constructor is also updated.

9.5.2 The Global Logger

In order to encourage the use of logging even in simple cases, the Logger class has a global logger instance. It was meant to be as easy as possible to use, so that you could always add trace statements as Logger.global.finest("x=" + x); instead of System.out.println("x=" + x);.

Unfortunately, that instance variable has to be initialized somewhere, and if other logging happens in the static initialization code, it was possible to cause deadlocks. Therefore, Logger.global was deprecated in Java 6. Instead, you were supposed to call Logger.getLogger(Logger.GLOBAL_LOGGER_NAME), which wasn't anyone's idea of quick and easy logging.

In Java 7, you can call Logger.getGlobal() instead, which isn't too bad.

9.5.3 Null Checks

The `Objects` class has methods `requireNonNull` for convenient null checks of parameters. Here is the simplest one:

```
public void process(String directions) {
    this.directions = Objects.requireNonNull(directions);
    ...
}
```

If `directions` is `null`, a `NullPointerException` is thrown, which doesn't seem like a huge improvement at first. But consider working back from a stack trace. When you see a call to `requireNonNull` as the culprit, you know right away what you did wrong.

You can also supply a message string for the exception:

```
this.directions = Objects.requireNonNull(directions,
    "directions must not be null");
```

9.5.4 ProcessBuilder

Prior to Java 5, the `Runtime.exec` method was the only way to execute an external command from within a Java application. Java 5 added the `ProcessBuilder` class that gives more control over the generated operating system process. In particular, with the `ProcessBuilder`, you can change the working directory.

Java 7 adds convenience methods to hook the standard input, output, and error streams of the process to files. For example,

```
ProcessBuilder builder = new ProcessBuilder(
    "grep", "-o", "[A-Za-z_][A-Za-z_0-9]*");
builder.redirectInput(Paths.get("Hello.java").toFile());
builder.redirectOutput(Paths.get("identifiers.txt").toFile());
Process process = builder.start();
process.waitFor();
```

 NOTE: Since Java 8, the `Process` class has a `waitFor` method with timeout:

```
boolean completed = process.waitFor(1, TimeUnit.MINUTES);
```

Also new in Java 7 is the `inheritIO` method of `ProcessBuilder`. It sets the standard input, output, and error streams of the process to those of the Java program. For example, when you run

```
ProcessBuilder builder = new ProcessBuilder("ls", "-al");
builder.inheritIO();
builder.start().waitFor();
```

then the output of the ls command is sent to System.out.

9.5.5 URLClassLoader

Suppose you want to write a Java program that automates execution of JUnit tests. To load the JUnitCore class, you need a class loader that reads the JUnit JAR files:

```
URL[] urls = {
    new URL("file:junit-4.11.jar"),
    new URL("file:hamcrest-core-1.3.jar")
};
URLClassLoader loader = new URLClassLoader(urls);
Class<?> klass = loader.loadClass("org.junit.runner.JUnitCore");
```

Before Java 7, code such as this could lead to resource leaks. Java 7 simply adds a close method to close the classloader. URLClassLoader now implements AutoCloseable, so you can use a try-with-resources statement:

```
try (URLClassLoader loader = new URLClassLoader(urls)) {
    Class<?> klass = loader.loadClass("org.junit.runner.JUnitCore");
    ...
}
```

 CAUTION: Don't use any classes after the classloader has been closed. If you do, and those classes need to load other classes to do their work, they will fail.

9.5.6 BitSet

A BitSet is a set of integers that is implemented as a sequence of bits. The ith bit is set if the set contains the integer i. That makes for very efficient set operations. Union/intersection/complement are simple bitwise or/and/not.

Java 7 adds methods to construct bitsets.

```
byte[] bytes = { (byte) 0b10101100, (byte) 0b00101000 };
BitSet primes = BitSet.valueOf(bytes);
    // {2, 3, 5, 7, 11, 13}
long[] longs = { 0x100010116L, 0x1L, 0x1L, 0L, 0x1L };
BitSet powersOfTwo = BitSet.valueOf(longs);
    // {1, 2, 4, 8, 16, 32, 64, 128, 256}
```

The inverse methods are toByteArray and toLongArray.

```
byte[] bytes = powersOfTwo.toByteArray();
    // [0b00010110, 1, 1, 0, 1, 0, 0, 0, 1, ...]
```

 NOTE: As of Java 8, BitSet has a method stream that yields an IntStream.

Exercises

1. Implement a code segment that constructs a Scanner and a PrintWriter at the end of Section 9.1.1, "The try-with-resources Statement," on page 180, without the try-with-resources statement. Be sure to close both objects, provided they have been properly constructed. You need to consider the following conditions:

    *   The Scanner constructor throws an exception.

    *   The PrintWriter constructor throws an exception.

    *   hasNext, next, or println throws an exception.

    *   in.close() throws an exception.

    *   out.close() throws an exception.

2. Improve on the preceding exercise by adding any exceptions thrown by in.close() or out.close() as suppressed exceptions to the original exception, if there was one.

3. When you rethrow an exception that you caught in a multi-catch clause, how do you declare its type in the throws declaration of the ambient method? For example, consider

    ```
    public void process() throws ... {
        try {
            ...
        catch (FileNotFoundException | UnknownHostException ex) {
            logger.log(Level.SEVERE, "...", ex);
            throw ex;
        }
    }
    ```

4. In which other parts of the Java library did you encounter situations that would benefit from multi-catch or, even better, common exception superclasses? (Hint: XML parsing.)

5. Write a program that reads all characters of a file and writes them out in reverse order. Use Files.readAllBytes and Files.write.

6. Write a program that reads all lines of a file and writes them out in reverse order. Use `Files.readAllLines` and `Files.write`.

7. Write a program that reads the contents of a web page and saves it to a file. Use `URL.openStream` and `Files.copy`.

8. Implement the `compareTo` method of the `Point` class in Section 9.3.3, "Comparing Numeric Types," on page 189, without using `Integer.compareTo`.

9. Given a class

```
public class LabeledPoint {
    private String label;
    private int x;
    private int y;

    ...
}
```

   implement the `equals` and `hashCode` methods.

10. Implement a `compareTo` method for the `LabeledPoint` class of the preceding exercise.

11. Using the `ProcessBuilder` class, write a program that calls `grep -r` to look for credit card numbers in all files in any subdirectory of the user's home directory. Collect the numbers that you found in a file.

12. Turn the application of the preceding exercise into an applet or a Java Web Start implementation. Suppose you want to offer it to users as a security scan. Package it so that it will run on your JRE. What did you have to do? What would your users have to do to run it from your web site?

Index